Michelle.Buchecker@sas.com

SQL Processing with SAS®

Course Notes

Michelle.Buchecker@sas.com

SQL Processing with SAS® Course Notes was developed by Jens Dahl Mikkelsen and Amy Peters. Additional contributions were made by Kathy Kiraly, Theresa Stemler, Rich Papel, and Roger Staum. Editing and Production support was provided by the Curriculum Development and Support Department.

SQL Processing with SAS® Course Notes

Book code E70256, course code SQL, prepared date 25Sep06.   SQL_003

ISBN 1-59994-251-8

Table of Contents

Course Description

This intermediate course focuses on using SQL as a data query and manipulation tool. You learn to use the SQL procedure as a data retrieval tool within SAS programs. Specifically, you learn how to perform queries on data; retrieve data from multiple tables; create views, indexes, and tables; and update or delete values in existing tables and views. Using features of the SQL procedure to debug, test, and optimize the performance of SQL queries is also discussed.

To learn more...

SAS Education

A full curriculum of general and statistical instructor-based training is available at any of the Institute's training facilities. Institute instructors can also provide on-site training.

For information on other courses in the curriculum, contact the SAS Education Division at 1-919-531-7321, or send e-mail to training@sas.com. You can also find this information on the Web at support.sas.com/training/ as well as in the Training Course Catalog.

SAS Publishing

For a list of other SAS books that relate to the topics covered in this Course Notes, USA customers can contact our SAS Publishing Department at 1-800-727-3228 or send e-mail to sasbook@sas.com. Customers outside the USA, please contact your local SAS office.

Also, see the Publications Catalog on the Web at support.sas.com/pubs for a complete list of books and a convenient order form.

Prerequisites

Before attending this course, you should be able to

- submit SAS programs on your operating system

- create and access SAS data sets

- use arithmetic, comparison, and logical operators

- invoke SAS procedures.

You can gain this experience from the *SAS Programming I: Essentials* course. No knowledge of SQL is necessary.

Chapter 1   Introduction

1.1 Structured Query Language

Objectives

- Understand the background and applications of Structured Query Language.

3

Structured Query Language

Structured Query Language (SQL)

- is a standardized language that is widely used to retrieve and update data in tables and in views based on those tables
- was originally designed as a query tool for relational databases, but it is now used by many software products.

4

Structured Query Language: Timeline

- 1970   Conceptualized and proposed by Dr. E. F. Codd at the IBM Research Laboratory, San Jose, CA
- 1970-1980   Developed by IBM
- 1981   First commercial SQL-based product, the IBM SQL/DS System
- 1989   Over 75 SQL database management systems exist, including SAS Release 6.06.

5

The SQL Procedure

The SQL procedure uses SQL to do the following:

- query SAS data sets
- generate reports from SAS data sets
- combine SAS data sets in many ways
- create and delete SAS data files, views, and indexes
- update existing SAS data sets

6

Structured Query Language

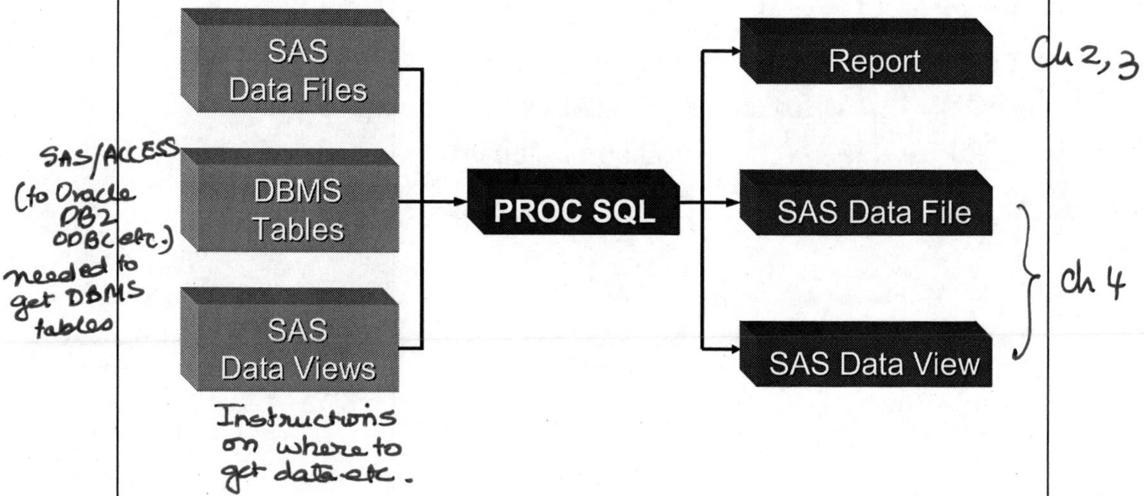
SAS
Data Files
DBMS
Tables
SAS
Data Views
PROC SQL
Report
SAS Data File
SAS Data View
Ch 2, 3
ch 4
SAS/ACCESS (to Oracle DB2 ODBC etc.) needed to get DBMS tables
Instructions on where to get data etc.

7

More About the SQL Procedure

The SQL procedure

- enables you to use SQL within SAS
- follows the guidelines set by the American National Standards Institute (ANSI)
- includes enhancements for compatibility with SAS software
- is part of Base SAS software
- can replace the need for multiple DATA and PROC steps with one query.

8

The SQL Procedure

IS NOT	IS
■ a replacement for the DATA step ■ a custom reporting tool.	■ a tool for queries ■ for data manipulation ■ an augmentation to the DATA step.

9

SAS Data Sets

A SAS data set can be a:

■ SAS data file that stores data descriptions and data values together

■ PROC SQL view that stores a PROC SQL query that retrieves data stored in other files

■ DATA step view that stores a DATA step that retrieves data stored in other files

■ SAS/ACCESS view that stores information required to retrieve data stored in a DBMS

View → instructions on where to get data

10

Terminology

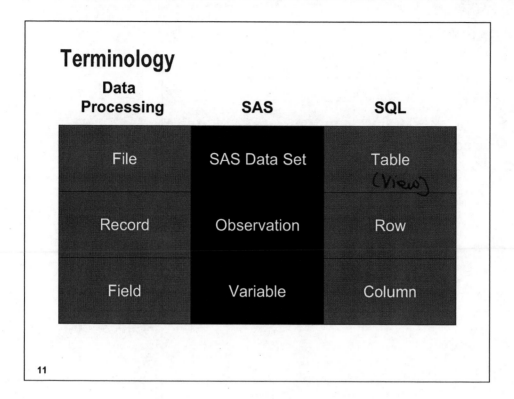

Data Processing	SAS	SQL
File	SAS Data Set	Table (View)
Record	Observation	Row
Field	Variable	Column

11

1.2 SAS Functions

Objectives

- Review the concatenation operator and various SAS functions.

13

SAS Numeric Functions

Example: Calculate age and create two new variables.

```
data new;
    date=today();
    birth='01jun1970'd;
    bmonth=month(birth);
    fullage=(date-birth)/365.25;
    age=int(fullage);
run;
proc print data=new noobs;
    format date birth date9.;
run;
```

- The TODAY function returns today's date as a SAS date value.
- The MONTH function returns the month portion of a SAS date as an integer, 1-12.
- The INT function returns the integer portion of a numeric value.

c1s2d01

14

SAS Numeric Functions

Output

```
                        The SAS System

          date        birth      bmonth    fullage     age

       12SEP2006    01JUN1970        6      36.2820      36
```

15

🖉   The results above were generated on September 22, 2006. Your values may differ.

SAS Character Functions

Use the SUBSTR function to extract individual characters from a character value.

General form of the SUBSTR function:

SUBSTR(*argument,position<,length>*)

argument   can be a character constant, variable, or expression.

position   specifies the starting position.

length   specifies the number of characters to extract. If omitted, the substring consists of the remainder of *argument*.

16

SAS Character Functions

Example: Create a full name from a character string.

```
data new;
   name='Gomez, Gabriela   ';
   fname1=substr(name,8)||' '||substr(name,1,5);
   fname2=trim(substr(name,8))||' '||substr(name,1,5);
run;
proc print data=new noobs;
run;
```

- SUBSTR extracts part of a character value. The length of the variable is determined by the first argument.
- TRIM removes trailing blanks from a value. The length of the variable is determined by the argument.
- || concatenates character values.

c1s2d02

17

SAS Character Functions

Output

```
                          The SAS System

           name              fname1              fname2

      Gomez, Gabriela     Gabriela   Gomez    Gabriela Gomez
```

18

SAS Character Functions

Use the SCAN function to extract the nth word of a character value.

General form of the SCAN function:

> **SCAN**(*argument,n<,delimiters>*)

argument   can be a character constant, variable, or expression.

n   specifies the nth word to extract from the argument.

delimiters defines characters that delimit (separate) words.

19

If the third argument is omitted, the default delimiters are

ASCII (PC, UNIX)	blank . < (+ | & ! $ *) ; - / , % ^
EBCDIC (z/OS)	blank . < (+ | & ! $ *) ; - / , % | ¢ ¬

SAS Character Functions

Example: Create a full name from a character string that
         contains a reversed name.

```
data new;
   name='Gomez, Gabriela   ';
   first=scan(name,2,',');
   last=scan(name,1,',');
   fname='Ms.'||trim(first)||' '||last;
proc print data=new noobs;
run;
```

SCAN returns a specific word from a character string.
The default length of the variable is 200.

c1s2d03

20

The above program creates FIRST and LAST columns using 200 bytes, which is the default length
returned from the SCAN function. To override this default, use a LENGTH statement, as shown below:

```
data new;
   length first last $20;
   name='Gomez, Gabriela   ';
   first=scan(name,2,',');
   last=scan(name,1,',');
   fname='Ms.'||trim(first)||' '||last;
run;
```

If the second argument of the SCAN function is a negative number, the function counts from the right
side of the text string instead of the left.

SAS Character Functions

Output

The SAS System			
name	first	last	fname
Gomez, Gabriela	Gabriela	Gomez	Ms. Gabriela Gomez

If the length of the variables `first` and `last` is 200,
where are the spaces?

21

1.3 Case Study

Objectives

- Explore the tables used in this course.

23

The examples and exercises in this course are based on the files of a fictitious airline company. These files include information on

- airline employees
- flights
- frequent flyers.

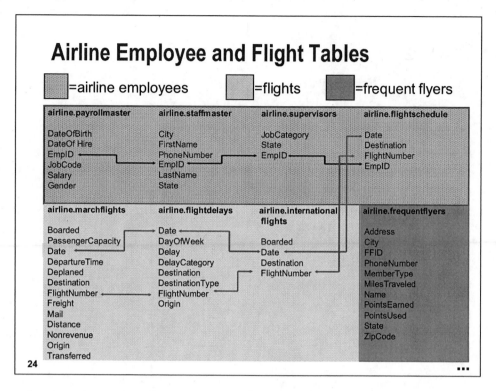

Airline Employee and Flight Tables

=airline employees   =flights   =frequent flyers

airline.payrollmaster

DateOfBirth
DateOf Hire
EmpID
JobCode
Salary
Gender

airline.staffmaster

City
FirstName
PhoneNumber
EmpID
LastName
State

airline.supervisors

JobCategory
State
EmpID

airline.flightschedule

Date
Destination
FlightNumber
EmpID

airline.marchflights

Boarded
PassengerCapacity
Date
DepartureTime
Deplaned
Destination
FlightNumber
Freight
Mail
Distance
Nonrevenue
Origin
Transferred

airline.flightdelays

Date
DayOfWeek
Delay
DelayCategory
Destination
DestinationType
FlightNumber
Origin

airline.international flights

Boarded
Date
Destination
FlightNumber

airline.frequentflyers

Address
City
FFID
PhoneNumber
MemberType
MilesTraveled
Name
PointsEarned
PointsUsed
State
ZipCode

24

Not all tables used in this class are shown above.

Airline Destination Codes and Descriptions

Code	Description
CPH	Copenhagen
DFW	Dallas/Ft. Worth
FRA	Frankfurt
LAX	Los Angeles
LGA	New York
LHR	London
ORD	Chicago
CDG	Paris
WAS	Washington
YYZ	Toronto

25

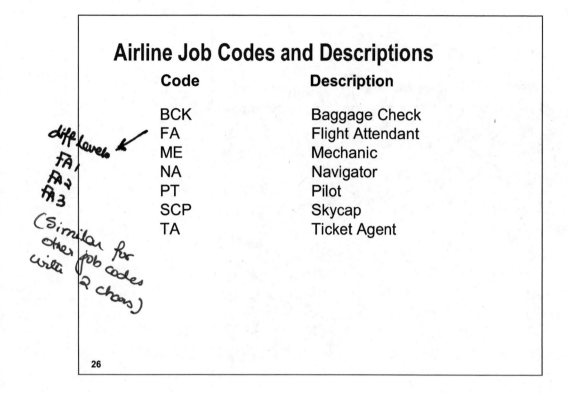

Airline Job Codes and Descriptions

Code	Description
BCK	Baggage Check
FA	Flight Attendant
ME	Mechanic
NA	Navigator
PT	Pilot
SCP	Skycap
TA	Ticket Agent

diff levels
FA 1
FA 2
FA 3

(Similar for other job codes with 2 chars)

26

1.4 Chapter Summary

Structured Query Language (SQL) is a standardized language that is widely used to retrieve and update data in tables and views based on those tables. The SQL procedure enables you to use SQL within SAS. You can use the SQL procedure to accomplish tasks such as querying SAS data sets, generating reports from SAS data sets, and combining SAS data sets.

The SQL procedure supports most of the functions available in the DATA step for data creation and manipulation. There are numeric functions to manipulate data values and character functions to manipulate character strings.

General form of the TODAY function:

> **TODAY( )**

General form of the MONTH function:

> **MONTH**(*SAS date value*)

General form of the INT function:

> **INT**(*numeric value)*

General form of the SUBSTR function:

> **SUBSTR**(*argument,position<,length>*)

General form of the TRIM function:

> **TRIM**(*argument*)

General form of the SCAN function:

> **SCAN**(*argument,n<,delimiters>*)

Chapter 2   Basic Queries

2.1   Overview of the SQL Procedure

Objectives

- Understand SQL procedure syntax.

3

Features of PROC SQL

- The PROC SQL statement does not need to be repeated with each query.
- Each statement is processed individually.
- No PROC PRINT step is needed to view query results.
- No PROC SORT step is needed to order query results.
- No RUN statement is needed.
- Use a QUIT statement to terminate PROC SQL.

4

SQL is a modular language because queries (or statements) are composed of smaller building blocks (or clauses).

The SELECT Statement

A SELECT statement is used to query one or more SAS data sets.

```
proc sql;
   select EmpID, JobCode, Salary
      from airline.payrollmaster
      where JobCode contains 'NA'
      order by Salary desc;
```

Only 2 clauses that are required

descending order.

c2s1d01

5

Use a comma to separate items in a list, such as column or table names. Place a single semicolon at the end of the last clause.

Features of the SELECT Statement

The features of the SELECT statement include the following:

- selects data that meets certain conditions
- groups data
- specifies an order for the data
- formats the data
- queries 1 to 32 tables

6

Table names can be 1 to 32 characters in length and are not case-sensitive.

Variable names can be 1 to 32 characters in length and are stored in mixed case but are normalized for lookups and comparisons. However, the first usage of the variable determines the capitalization pattern.

Librefs and filerefs are limited to 8 characters. Starting in SAS®9, format and informat names can be up to 32 characters in length.

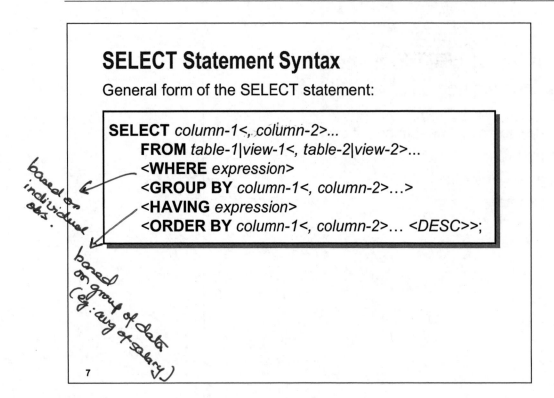

SELECT Statement Syntax

General form of the SELECT statement:

SELECT *column-1<, column-2>...*
    FROM *table-1|view-1<, table-2|view-2>...*
    <WHERE *expression>*
    <GROUP BY *column-1<, column-2>...>*
    <HAVING *expression>*
    <ORDER BY *column-1<, column-2>... <DESC>>;*

based on individual obs.

based on group of data (eg.: avg of salary)

7

SELECT   specifies the columns to be selected.

FROM   specifies the table to be queried.

WHERE   subsets the data based on a condition.

GROUP BY   classifies the data into groups.

HAVING   subsets groups of data based on a group condition.

ORDER BY   sorts rows by the values of specific columns. By default, results are sorted in ascending order. Use the DESC keyword to sort in descending order.

✎   The order of the above clauses within the SELECT statement **does** matter.

table   is a SAS data set (data file or data view).

column   is a column name, expression, or summary function.

The VALIDATE Keyword

Partial SAS Log

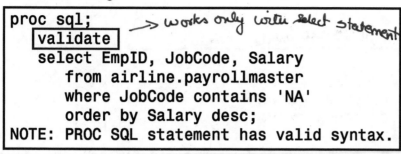

```
proc sql;
   validate
   select EmpID, JobCode, Salary
      from airline.payrollmaster
      where JobCode contains 'NA'
      order by Salary desc;
NOTE: PROC SQL statement has valid syntax.
```

→ works only with select statement

c2s1d02

8

Features of the VALIDATE Keyword

The features of the VALIDATE keyword include the following:

- is used only in a SELECT statement
- tests the syntax of a query without executing the query
- checks column name validity
- prints error messages for invalid queries

9

The NOEXEC Option

The NOEXEC option can also be used for syntax checking.

Partial SAS Log   → *Syntax chk mode*

```
proc sql noexec;
    select EmpID,JobCode,Salary
        from airline.payrollmaster
        where JobCode contains 'NA'
        order by Salary desc;
NOTE:Statement not executed due to NOEXEC option.
```

c2s1d03

10

Don't really need validate statement when using SAS SQL

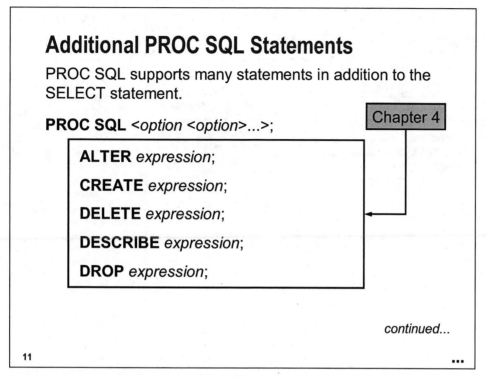

Additional PROC SQL Statements

PROC SQL supports many statements in addition to the SELECT statement.

PROC SQL *<option <option>...>*;

Chapter 4

ALTER *expression*;

CREATE *expression*;

DELETE *expression*;

DESCRIBE *expression*;

DROP *expression*;

continued...

11

ALTER	adds, drops, and modifies columns in a table.
CREATE	builds new tables.
DELETE	eliminates unwanted rows from a table or view.
DESCRIBE	displays table attributes or view definitions.
DROP	eliminates entire tables, views, or indexes.

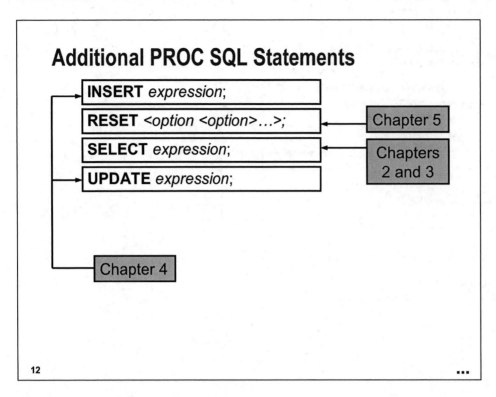

INSERT   adds rows of data to tables.

RESET   adds to or changes PROC SQL options without re-invoking the procedure.

SELECT   specifies columns to be printed.

UPDATE   modifies data values in existing rows of a table or view.

The NOEXEC option checks for invalid syntax in all the statements previously mentioned, but the VALIDATE option applies only to the SELECT statement.

2.2 Specifying Columns

Objectives

- Display columns directly from a table.
- Display columns calculated from other columns in a query.

14

Retrieving Data from a Table

If you are familiar with a table, you can specify column names to be printed in the SELECT statement.

Example: Print employee IDs, job codes, and salaries.

```
proc sql;
    select EmpID, JobCode, Salary
        from airline.payrollmaster;
```

→ (obs=10) if we want only 10 obs.

Can use ods destinations to output html etc.

typical data set options used in Parentheses can be used next to data set name in from clause.

15   c2s2d01

Starting with SAS®9, you can reference tables using their physical filename:

```
proc sql;
   select *
   from 'c:\workshop\winsas\sql\payrollmaster.sas7bdat';
quit;
```

Employee IDs, Job Codes, and Salaries

Partial Output

```
              The SAS System
        Emp    Job
        ID     Code      Salary

        1919   TA2      $48,126
        1653   ME2      $49,151
        1400   ME1      $41,677
        1350   FA3      $46,040
        1401   TA3      $54,351
        1499   ME3      $60,235
        1101   SCP      $26,212
        1333   PT2     $124,048
        1402   TA2      $45,661
```

16

Retrieving Data from a Table

```
proc sql;
    select  *
        from airline.payrollmaster;
```

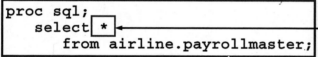

If you are not familiar with a table, an asterisk in the SELECT statement prints all columns in their originally stored order.

Partial Output

```
                      The SAS System

      Emp              Job
      ID    Gender    Code    Salary    DateOfBirth   DateOfHire

      1919    M        TA2    $48,126    16SEP1958    07JUN1985
      1653    F        ME2    $49,151    19OCT1962    12AUG1988
      1400    M        ME1    $41,677    08NOV1965    19OCT1988
      1350    F        FA3    $46,040    04SEP1963    01AUG1988
      1401    M        TA3    $54,351    16DEC1948    21NOV1983
      1499    M        ME3    $60,235    29APR1952    11JUN1978
```

c2s2d02

17

The FEEDBACK Option

Use the FEEDBACK option to write the expanded
SELECT statement to the SAS log.

Partial SAS Log

```
proc sql feedback;
    select *
        from airline.payrollmaster;
NOTE: Statement transforms to      ⁊col name
        select PAYROLLMASTER.EmpID,
                PAYROLLMASTER.Gender, PAYROLLMASTER.JobCode,
                PAYROLLMASTER.Salary,
                PAYROLLMASTER.DateOfBirth,
                PAYROLLMASTER.DateOfHire
            from AIRLINE.PAYROLLMASTER;
```
table name

c2s2d03

18

 This option expands any use of an asterisk into the list of qualified columns it represents. NOFEEDBACK is the default.

Expressions

Calculate new columns from existing columns, and name
the new columns using the AS keyword.

Example: Calculate employee bonuses.

```
proc sql;
    select EmpID, JobCode, Salary,
            Salary * .10 as Bonus
        from airline.payrollmaster;
```

c2s2d04

19

The new column is called an *alias*. The AS keyword is required. Omission of the alias causes the column heading to be blank.

Employee Bonuses

Partial Output

```
                    The SAS System

        Emp    Job
        ID     Code     Salary      Bonus

        1919   TA2     $48,126     4812.64
        1653   ME2     $49,151     4915.12
        1400   ME1     $41,677     4167.66
        1350   FA3     $46,040     4604.04
        1401   TA3     $54,351     5435.08
        1499   ME3     $60,235      6023.5
        1101   SCP     $26,212     2621.22
        1333   PT2    $124,048    12404.84
        1402   TA2     $45,661      4566.1
        1479   TA3     $54,299      5429.9
        1403   ME1     $39,301     3930.08
        1739   PT1     $93,124     9312.38
        1658   SCP     $25,120     2512.02
```

20

Expressions

Use SAS DATA step functions for calculating columns.

Example: Calculate the age of each employee.

```
proc sql;
   select EmpID, JobCode,
          int((today()-DateOfBirth)/365.25)
          as Age
      from airline.payrollmaster;
```

21   c2s2d05

Employee Ages

Partial Output

```
          The SAS System

     Emp   Job
     ID    Code        Age
     ─────────────────────────
     1919  TA2          47
     1653  ME2          43
     1400  ME1          40
     1350  FA3          43
     1401  TA3          57
```

22

All SAS DATA step functions are supported except LAG and DIF.

2.3   Specifying Rows

Objectives

- Eliminate duplicate rows in a query.
- Subset the data displayed in a query.

24

Specifying All Rows in a Table

By default, all rows in a table are returned in a query.

Example: Display all rows and columns of the
airline.internationalflights
table.

```
proc sql;
   select *
      from airline.internationalflights;
```

c2s3d01

25

All Rows in a Table

Partial Output

```
                        The SAS System

     FlightNumber      Date      Destination      Boarded

         182        01MAR2000      YYZ              104
         219        01MAR2000      LHR              198
         387        01MAR2000      CPH              152
         622        01MAR2000      FRA              207
         821        01MAR2000      LHR              205
         132        01MAR2000      YYZ              115
         271        01MAR2000      CDG              138
         182        02MAR2000      YYZ              116
         219        02MAR2000      LHR              147
         387        02MAR2000      CPH              105
         622        02MAR2000      FRA              176
         821        02MAR2000      LHR              201
         132        02MAR2000      YYZ              106
```

26

Eliminating Duplicate Rows

Use the DISTINCT keyword to eliminate duplicate rows in query results.

Example: Determine the international flights that were flown during the month.

```
proc sql;
   select distinct FlightNumber,
            Destination
        from airline.internationalflights;
```

27   c2s3d02

   The DISTINCT keyword applies to all columns in the SELECT list. One row is displayed for each existing combination of values.

Eliminating Duplicate Rows

Output

```
                The SAS System

        FlightNumber Destination

            132          YYZ
            182          YYZ
            219          LHR
            271          CDG
            387          CPH
            622          FRA
            821          LHR
```

28

Subsetting with the WHERE Clause

Use a WHERE clause to specify a condition that the data
must satisfy before being selected.

Example: Display all employees that earn more than
           $112,000.

```
proc sql;
   select EmpID,JobCode,Salary
      from airline.payrollmaster
      where Salary > 112000;
```

c2s3d03

29

Subsetting with the WHERE Clause

Output

```
                 The SAS System

        Emp    Job
        ID     Code      Salary
        ───────────────────────────
        1333   PT2     $124,048
        1404   PT2     $127,926
        1118   PT3     $155,931
        1410   PT2     $118,559
        1777   PT3     $153,482
        1106   PT2     $125,485
        1442   PT2     $118,350
        1478   PT2     $117,884
        1890   PT2     $120,254
        1107   PT2     $125,968
        1830   PT2     $118,259
        1928   PT2     $125,801
```

30

Subsetting with the WHERE Clause

You can use all common comparison operators in a WHERE clause.

Mnemonic	Symbol	Definition
LT	<	Less than
GT	>	Greater than
EQ	=	Equal to
LE	<=	Less than or equal to
GE	>=	Greater than or equal to
NE	¬=	Not equal to (EBCDIC)
	^=	Not equal to (ASCII)

31

Subsetting with the WHERE Clause

You can use the IN operator to compare a value to a list of values. If the value matches at least one in the list, the expression is true; otherwise, the expression is false.

```
where JobCategory in ('PT','NA','FA')
```

```
where DayOfWeek in (2,4,6)
```

32

Subsetting with the WHERE Clause

You can specify multiple expressions in a WHERE clause by using logical operators.

Mnemonic	Symbol	Definition
OR	|	or, either
AND	&	and, both
NOT	¬	not, negation EBCDIC
NOT	^	not, negation ASCII

33

Subsetting with the WHERE Clause

Use either **CONTAINS** or **?** to select rows that include the substring specified.

```
where word ? 'LAM'
```

(BLAME, LAMENT, and BEDLAM are selected.)

Use either **IS NULL** or **IS MISSING** to select rows with missing values.

```
where FlightNumber is missing
```

Also con use.

IS NOT NULL

IS NOT MISSING

34

Alternative statements are

- **where FlightNumber = ' '**
- **where FlightNumber = .**

With the = operator, you must know whether **FlightNumber** is character or numeric. However, if you use IS MISSING, you do not need advance knowledge of the column type.

Subsetting with the WHERE Clause

Use **BETWEEN-AND** to select rows containing ranges of values, inclusively.

```
where Date between '01mar2000'd
      and '07mar2000'd
```

```
where Salary between 70000 and 80000
```

35

Subsetting with the WHERE Clause

Use **LIKE** to select rows by comparing character values to specified patterns.

A % sign replaces any number of characters.

```
where LastName like 'H%'
```

(H plus any characters; for example, HENDRY, HANSON, and HALL are selected.)

36

Subsetting with the WHERE Clause

A single underscore ('_') replaces individual characters.

```
where JobCode like ' __1
```

captures any two characters and 1, for example, 'FA1', 'TA1', 'NA1'.

Two underscores, followed by a 1

37

Subsetting with the WHERE Clause

Select the jobcodes that contain an underscore (_), followed by a number.

```
proc sql;
    select EmpID, Jobcode
        from airline.payrollmaster2
        where jobcode like 'FA_%';
quit;
```

Partial Output
(rows 7-13)

Emp ID	Jobcode
5098	FA_2
1124	FA_1
1422	FA_1
1094	FA_1
6345	FAN2
7109	FAN2
1113	FA_1

c2s3d04

38

ESCAPE Clause

The ESCAPE clause in the LIKE condition enables you to designate a single character string literal, known as an *escape character*, to indicate how PROC SQL should interpret the LIKE wildcards, percent (%) and underscore (_), if they are used within a character string.

Escape only available in SQL

39

ESCAPE Clause

```
proc sql;
   select EmpID, Jobcode
      from airline.payrollmaster2
      where jobcode like 'FA/_%' ESCAPE '/';
quit;
```

Partial Output
(rows 7-15)

Emp ID	Jobcode
5098	FA_2
1124	FA_1
1422	FA_1
1094	FA_1
1113	FA_1
8322	FA_2
1103	FA_1
1477	FA_2
1115	FA_3

c2s3d05

40

Subsetting with the WHERE Clause

The sounds-like (=*) operator selects rows containing
a spelling variation of the specified word(s).

```
where LastName =* 'SMITH'
```

selects values SMITT, SMYTHE, and SMOTHE, in
addition to SMITH.

41

Subsetting with Calculated Values

Because a WHERE clause is evaluated first, columns
used in the WHERE clause must exist in the table or
be derived from existing columns.

Execution order
① From
② where

42

Subsetting with Calculated Values

Example: Display only the flights where the total number
of passengers was fewer than 100 people.

```
proc sql;
   select FlightNumber,Date,Destination,
          Boarded + Transferred + Nonrevenue
          as Total
      from airline.marchflights        ← exec 1
      where Total < 100;               ← exec 2
```

*but total in
select not yet
calculated*

c2s3d06

43

Subsetting with Calculated Values

Partial Log

```
ERROR: The following columns were not
found in the contributing tables: Total.
```

44

Subsetting with Calculated Values

One solution is to repeat the calculation in the
WHERE clause.

```
proc sql;
   select FlightNumber, Date, Destination,
          Boarded+Transferred+Nonrevenue
          as Total
      from airline.marchflights
      where Boarded+Transferred+Nonrevenue < 100;
```

45

c2s3d07

Subsetting with Calculated Values

A more efficient method is to use the CALCULATED
keyword to refer to already calculated columns in the
SELECT clause.

```
proc sql;
   select FlightNumber, Date, Destination,
          Boarded + Transferred + Nonrevenue
          as Total
      from airline.marchflights
      where calculated Total < 100;
```

46

c2s3d08

Subsetting with Calculated Values

Partial Output

```
                    The SAS System

FlightNumber      Date    Destination     Total

982            01MAR2000   DFW              70
416            01MAR2000   WAS              93
829            01MAR2000   WAS              96
416            02MAR2000   WAS              90
302            02MAR2000   WAS              93
```

47

Subsetting with Calculated Values

You can also use the CALCULATED keyword in other parts of a query, for example, in a SELECT clause.

```
proc sql;
   select FlightNumber, Date, Destination,
          Boarded + Transferred + Nonrevenue
          as Total,
       calculated Total/2 as half
       from airline.marchflights;
```

c2s3d09

48

Subsetting with Calculated Values

Partial Output

```
                         The SAS System

FlightNumber       Date  Destination   Total    half

182           01MAR2000  YYZ             123    61.5
114           01MAR2000  LAX             196      98
202           01MAR2000  ORD             167    83.5
219           01MAR2000  LHR             222     111
439           01MAR2000  LAX             185    92.5
387           01MAR2000  CPH             163    81.5
290           01MAR2000  WAS             119    59.5
```

49

2.4 Presenting Data

Objectives

- Order the data displayed in a query.
- Use SAS formats, labels, and titles to enhance query output.

51

Ordering Data

Use the ORDER BY clause to sort query results in

- ascending order (the default)
- descending order by following the column name with the DESC keyword.

52

Ordering Data

```
proc sql;
   select EmpID,JobCode,Salary
      from airline.payrollmaster
      where JobCode contains 'NA'
      order by Salary desc;
```

c2s4d01

53

You can specify the collating sequence by using the SORTSEQ= option in the PROC SQL statement. Use this option only if you want a collating sequence other than your system's or installation's default collating sequence. For additional information, see SORTSEQ under the SORT procedure in your online or written documentation.

PROC SQL uses information provided by a table's internal sort indicator (if available) to avoid performing unnecessary sorts.

Ordering Data

Output

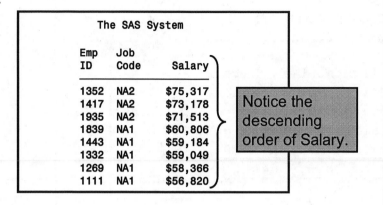

```
                The SAS System

        Emp   Job
        ID    Code     Salary

        1352  NA2     $75,317
        1417  NA2     $73,178
        1935  NA2     $71,513
        1839  NA1     $60,806
        1443  NA1     $59,184
        1332  NA1     $59,049
        1269  NA1     $58,366
        1111  NA1     $56,820
```

Notice the descending order of Salary.

54

Ordering Data

In an ORDER BY clause, you order query results by specifying the following:

- any column or expression (display or nondisplay)
- a column name or a number that represents the position of an item in the SELECT list
- multiple columns

55

Ordering Data

Example: Display the London flights in date order by
descending total number of passengers.

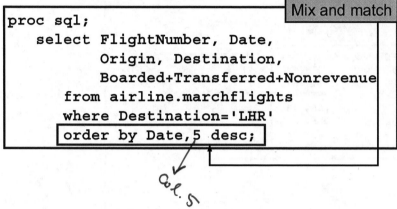

```
proc sql;
    select FlightNumber, Date,
           Origin, Destination,
           Boarded+Transferred+Nonrevenue
    from airline.marchflights
    where Destination='LHR'
    order by Date, 5 desc;
```

Mix and match

col. 5

56   c2s4d02

Ordering Data

Partial Output

		The SAS System		
FlightNumber	Date	Origin	Destination	
219	01MAR2000	LGA	LHR	222
821	01MAR2000	LGA	LHR	222
821	02MAR2000	LGA	LHR	210
219	02MAR2000	LGA	LHR	172
219	03MAR2000	LGA	LHR	211
821	03MAR2000	LGA	LHR	172
219	04MAR2000	LGA	LHR	250
821	04MAR2000	LGA	LHR	182
219	05MAR2000	LGA	LHR	167
821	06MAR2000	LGA	LHR	185
219	06MAR2000	LGA	LHR	183

57

Enhancing Query Output

You can use SAS formats and labels to customize PROC SQL output. After the column name in the SELECT list, you specify the following:

- LABEL= option to alter the column heading
- FORMAT= option to alter the appearance of the values in that column.

58

The LABEL, FORMAT, INFORMAT, and LENGTH options are not part of the ANSI standard, but are SAS enhancements.

Enhancing Query Output

Example: Enhance the report. Display the navigators and their salaries.

```
proc sql;
   select EmpID label='Employee Identifier',
          JobCode label='Job Code',
          Salary label='Annual Salary'
                 format=dollar12.2
      from airline.payrollmaster
      where JobCode contains 'NA'
      order by Salary desc;
```

c2s4d03

59

Enhanced Query Output

Output

```
                    The SAS System

        Employee     Job          Annual
        Identifier   Code         Salary

        1352         NA2       $75,317.20
        1417         NA2       $73,178.00
        1935         NA2       $71,513.40
        1839         NA1       $60,806.20
        1443         NA1       $59,183.60
        1332         NA1       $59,049.20
        1269         NA1       $58,366.00
        1111         NA1       $56,820.40
```

60

To force PROC SQL to ignore permanent labels in a table, specify the NOLABEL system option.

Enhancing Query Output

Here are examples of enhancing output:

- define a column containing a character constant by placing a text string in the SELECT list
- use SAS titles and footnotes to enhance the query's appearance

61

Enhancing Query Output

Example: Display bonus values for all flight engineers.

```
proc sql;
title 'Current Bonus Information';
title2 'Navigators - All Levels';
   select EmpID
          label='Employee Identifier',
          'bonus is:',
          Salary *.05 format=dollar12.2
      from airline.payrollmaster
      where JobCode contains 'NA'
      order by Salary desc;
```

c2s4d04

62

TITLE and FOOTNOTE statements must precede the SELECT statement.

Also, a column of numeric values can be defined in a way similar to the above character constant `'bonus is:'`.

Enhancing Query Output

Output

```
              Current Bonus Information
               Navigators - All Levels

       Employee
       Identifier

       1352       bonus is:     $3,765.86
       1417       bonus is:     $3,658.90
       1935       bonus is:     $3,575.67
       1839       bonus is:     $3,040.31
       1443       bonus is:     $2,959.18
       1332       bonus is:     $2,952.46
       1269       bonus is:     $2,918.30
       1111       bonus is:     $2,841.02
```

63

Exercises

Submit a LIBNAME statement to assign the libref **airline** to the SAS data library for this course.

TSO: `libname airline '.sql.sasdata';`

Directory-based systems: `libname airline '.';`

1. **Querying a Table**

    a. Submit a PROC SQL query that displays all rows and all columns of **airline.payrollmaster**.

    b. Recall the previous query and alter it so that only the columns for employee ID, gender, job code, and salary are displayed.

    c. Recall the previous query and alter it so that a new column is displayed as one third of the employee's salary. Name the new column **Tax**.

    d. Recall the previous query and alter it so that the Tax and Salary columns are displayed with commas and two decimal places.

    e. Recall the previous query and alter it so that only male employees are listed.

    f. Recall the previous query and alter it so that only male flight attendants are displayed.

2. **Eliminating Duplicates**

    Use the **airline.staffmaster** table to create a report that displays the cities where airline employees reside. The report must contain only one row per city, be ordered by city, and have an appropriate title.

```
                     Cities Where Employees Live

             City
             _____

             BRIDGEPORT
             MT. VERNON
             NEW YORK
             PATERSON
             PRINCETON
             STAMFORD
             WHITE PLAINS
```

3. Subsetting Data

Use the `airline.marchflights` table to create a report that shows all flights whose total number of passengers is less than one third of the airplane's capacity. Display the flights in descending number of total passengers. Create an appropriate title.

✏ Total is the sum of **Boarded**, **Transferred** and **Nonrevenue**.

```
              Flights Less Than One Third Full


                                          Passenger
    FlightNumber      Date  Destination   Total   Capacity

       290      19MAR2000  WAS            59        180
       523      05MAR2000  ORD            59        210
       290      05MAR2000  WAS            55        180
       183      19MAR2000  WAS            53        180
       982      12MAR2000  DFW            49        180
       183      25MAR2000  WAS            43        180
       302      31MAR2000  WAS            34        180
       302      22MAR2000  WAS            33        180
       416      05MAR2000  WAS            31        180
       872      21MAR2000  LAX             .        210
       921      27MAR2000  DFW             .        180
```

4. Querying Data (Optional)

A customer service representative must contact a person in the frequent flyer table, but the service representative only remembers that the person's first name begins with an N. Use the `airline.frequentflyers` table to list the names of all possible people.

```
    Frequent Fliers with First Names Beginning with an 'N'


                              Frequent
              Name            FlyerNumber

          CARAWAY, NEIL       WD4762
          CHAPMAN, NEIL       WD8968
          OVERBY, NADINE      WD5201
          WILDER, NEIL        WD6169
          JONES, NATHAN       WD1961
          TUCKER, NEIL        WD2719
          WELLS, NADINE       WD6504
          SANDERSON, NATHAN   WD7916
```

5. Using SAS Functions (Optional)

Query the **airline.payrollmaster** table to determine how old each employee was when the employee was hired. Display the employee's ID, birth date, hire date, and age at time of employment. Format the two dates with the MMDDYY10. format and label each column appropriately.

Partial Output

```
                    Employee Age Information

        Employee                             Age At
        ID        Birth Date   Hire Date   Employment
        ───────────────────────────────────────────────

        1919      09/16/1958   06/07/1985      26
        1653      10/19/1962   08/12/1988      25
        1400      11/08/1965   10/19/1988      22
        1350      09/04/1963   08/01/1988      24
        1401      12/16/1948   11/21/1983      34
        1499      04/29/1952   06/11/1978      26
        1101      06/09/1960   10/04/1988      28
        1333      04/03/1959   02/14/1979      19
```

2.5 Summarizing Data

Objectives

■ Use functions to summarize data in a query.

66

Summary Functions

Example: Find the total number of passengers for
          each flight in March.

```
proc sql;
   select Date, FlightNumber, Boarded,
          Transferred, Nonrevenue,
          sum(Boarded,Transferred,Nonrevenue)
          as Total
          from airline.marchflights;
```

This calculation
is performed *across
columns*
for each row.

c2s5d01

67

Summary Function

```
                    The SAS System

          Flight
   Date   Number  Boarded  Transferred  Nonrevenue  Total

01MAR2000  182     104          16            3       123
01MAR2000  114     172          18            6       196
01MAR2000  202     151          11            5       167
01MAR2000  219     198          17            7       222
01MAR2000  439     167          13            5       185
01MAR2000  387     152           8            3       163
01MAR2000  290      96    +      16    +       7   =   119
```

If you specify more than one column name in a summary function, the function acts like a DATA step function. The calculation is performed for each row.

68

Summary Functions

If you specify only one column name in a summary function, the statistic is calculated down the column.

Example: Determine the average salary
             for the company.

```
proc sql;
   select avg(Salary) as MeanSalary
      from airline.payrollmaster;
```

69   c2s5d02

Summary Function

Data set `airline.payrollmaster`

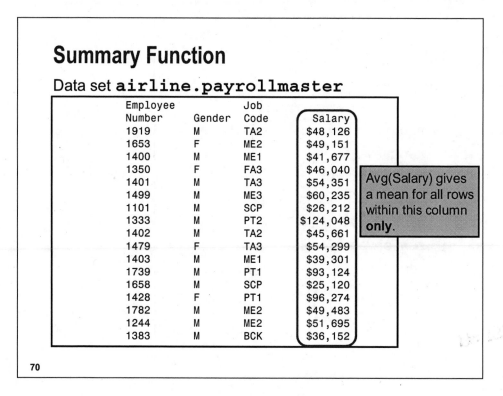

Employee Number	Gender	Job Code	Salary
1919	M	TA2	$48,126
1653	F	ME2	$49,151
1400	M	ME1	$41,677
1350	F	FA3	$46,040
1401	M	TA3	$54,351
1499	M	ME3	$60,235
1101	M	SCP	$26,212
1333	M	PT2	$124,048
1402	M	TA2	$45,661
1479	F	TA3	$54,299
1403	M	ME1	$39,301
1739	M	PT1	$93,124
1658	M	SCP	$25,120
1428	F	PT1	$96,274
1782	M	ME2	$49,483
1244	M	ME2	$51,695
1383	M	BCK	$36,152

Avg(Salary) gives a mean for all rows within this column **only**.

70

This is comparable to a SAS procedure (for example, the MEANS procedure), which computes statistics on table columns.

Summary Functions

Output

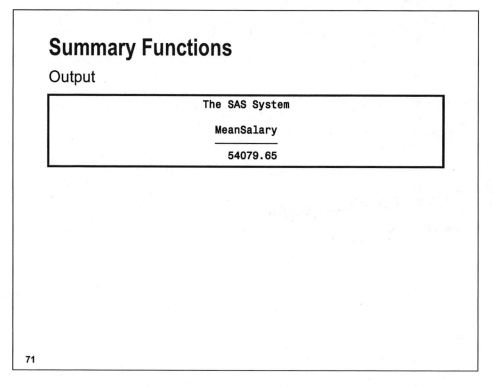

```
            The SAS System

            MeanSalary
            ──────────
            54079.65
```

71

The SQL procedure supports numerous functions for calculating statistics. Some functions have more than one name to accommodate both SAS and SQL conventions.

Summary Functions

The following are selected functions:

(AVG) MEAN	mean or average value
(COUNT) FREQ, N	number of nonmissing values
(MAX)	largest value
(MIN)	smallest value
NMISS	number of missing values
STD	standard deviation
(SUM)	sum of values
VAR	variance

Circled are ANSI std
Rest are SAS

72

Summary Functions

Example: Add the JobCode column to the summarized
          query.

```
proc sql;
   select JobCode, avg(Salary) as average
      from airline.payrollmaster;
```

log note
'Remerge of summary stats occured !
Usually not what you want

73   c2s5d03

Summary Functions

Partial Output

```
                   The SAS System

              Job
              Code    average
              ─────────────────
              TA2     54079.65
              ME2     54079.65
              ME1     54079.65
              FA3     54079.65
              TA3     54079.65
              ME3     54079.65
              SCP     54079.65
              PT2     54079.65
              TA2     54079.65
              TA3     54079.65
              ME1     54079.65
```

74

✎   By default, summary functions calculate statistics based on the entire table. The average is calculated and then re-merged with the individual rows in the table.

How can you find the average salary for each job code?

Grouping Data

You can use the GROUP BY clause to

- classify the data into groups based on the values of one or more columns
- calculate statistics for each unique value of the grouping columns.

75

Grouping Data

Example: Display the average salary for each job code.

```
proc sql;
   select JobCode, avg(Salary) as
          average format=dollar11.2
      from airline.payrollmaster
      group by JobCode;
```

c2s5d04

76

Grouping Data

Partial Output

```
The SAS System

Job
Code      average
_____

BCK     $36,111.91
FA1     $32,255.11
FA2     $39,181.63
FA3     $46,107.40
ME1     $39,900.35
ME2     $49,807.60
ME3     $59,375.00
NA1     $58,845.08
NA2     $73,336.20
PT1     $95,071.20
PT2    $122,253.60
PT3    $154,706.30
SCP     $25,632.40
```

77

Analyzing Groups of Data

The COUNT(*) summary function counts the number of rows.

Example: Determine the total number of employees.

```
proc sql;
    select count(*) as count
        from airline.payrollmaster;
```

Output

```
            The SAS System

                count
              _____

                 148
```

c2s5d05

78

The COUNT function is the only function that allows an asterisk (*) as an argument.

Analyzing Groups of Data

Example: Determine the total number of employees
          within each job category.

```
proc sql;
    select substr(JobCode,1,2)
           label='Job Category',
           count(*) as count
        from airline.payrollmaster
        group by 1;
```

c2s5d06

79

Analyzing Groups of Data

Output

```
                    The SAS System

            Job
            Category      count
            ─────────────────────
            BC                9
            FA               34
            ME               29
            NA                8
            PT               20
            SC                7
            TA               41
```

80

Analyzing Groups of Data

Example: Calculate each navigator's salary as
          a percentage of all navigators' salaries.

```
proc sql;
  ③select EmpID, Salary,
         (Salary/sum(Salary)) as percent
         format=percent8.2
    ① from airline.payrollmaster
    ② where JobCode contains 'NA';
```

81

c2s5d07

Analyzing Groups of Data

Output

```
                    The SAS System
          Emp
          ID       Salary    percent
          ───────────────────────────
          1269    $58,366    11.35%
          1935    $71,513    13.91%
          1417    $73,178    14.23%
          1839    $60,806    11.82%
          1111    $56,820    11.05%
          1352    $75,317    14.65%
          1332    $59,049    11.48%
          1443    $59,184    11.51%
```

82

PROC SQL automatically re-merges the summary statistic with the table to calculate the percentage. This requires two passes through the data: one to compute the column sum and another to compute each row's percentage of the total. A note appears in the SAS log when re-merging occurs.

Partial Log

```
NOTE: The query requires remerging summary statistics back with the original data.
```

Selecting Groups of Data with the HAVING Clause

The WHERE clause selects data based on values for individual rows. To select entire groups of data, use the HAVING clause.

Example: Display all job codes with an average salary of more than $56,000.

```
proc sql;
  ③select JobCode, avg(Salary) as average
       format=dollar11.2
    ② from airline.payrollmaster
    ① group by JobCode
    ④  having avg(Salary) > 56000 ;
```

83   c2s5d08

Alternatively, you can code the HAVING clause as follows: (since having executes last)

```
having average > 56000;
having calculated average > 56000;
```

Selecting Groups of Data with the HAVING Clause

Output

```
                The SAS System

        Job
        Code        average

        ME3      $59,375.00
        NA1      $58,845.08
        NA2      $73,336.20
        PT1      $95,071.20
        PT2     $122,253.60
        PT3     $154,706.30
```

84

2.6 Subqueries

Objectives

- Describe how to subset data based on values returned from other queries.
- Explain the difference between a correlated and noncorrelated subquery.

86

Subqueries

Subqueries have the following characteristics:

- are inner queries that return values to be used by an outer query to complete a subsetting expression in a WHERE or HAVING clause
- return single or multiple values to be used by the outer query
- can return only a single column

87

Subqueries are also known as nested queries, inner queries, and sub-selects.

Subqueries: Noncorrelated

Example: Display job codes where the group's average
          salary exceeds the company's average salary.

```
proc sql;
   select JobCode,avg(Salary) as MeanSalary
      from airline.payrollmaster
      group by JobCode
      having avg(Salary) >
            (select avg(Salary)
             from airline.payrollmaster);
```

Then pass results
to outer query

Evaluate
first

This can be run by itself

88   c2s6d01
                                        •••

Subqueries: Noncorrelated

After the subquery executes, the outer query code
resolves to:

```
proc sql;
   select JobCode,avg(Salary) as MeanSalary
      from airline.payrollmaster
      group by JobCode
      having avg(Salary) > (54079.65);
```

89

Subqueries: Noncorrelated

Output

```
              The SAS System

       Job
       Code    MeanSalary

       ME3         59375
       NA1      58845.08
       NA2       73336.2
       PT1       95071.2
       PT2      122253.6
       PT3      154706.3
       TA3      55551.42
```

90

Subqueries: Noncorrelated

Example: Send birthday cards to employees with
          February birthdays. Names and addresses
          are in **airline.staffmaster**, and birth
          dates are in **airline.payrollmaster**.

```
proc sql;
    select EmpID, LastName, FirstName,
        City, State
        from airline.staffmaster
        where EmpID in
            (select EmpID
             from airline.payrollmaster
             where month(DateOfBirth)=2);
```

c2s6d02

91

Noncorrelated Subqueries: How Do They Work?

airline.payrollmaster
Partial Listing

```
proc sql;
    select EmpID, LastName,
       FirstName, City, State
    from airline.staffmaster
    where EmpID in
       (select EmpID
        from airline.payrollmaster
        where month(DateOfBirth)=2);
```

EmpID	DateOfBirth
. . .	. . .
1038	11/13/1967
1420	02/23/1963
1561	12/03/1961
1434	07/14/1960
1414	03/28/1970
1112	12/03/1962
1390	02/23/1963
1332	09/20/1968
. . .	. . .

Step 1: Evaluate the inner query and build a virtual table that satisfies the WHERE criteria.

92

c2s6d02

Noncorrelated Subqueries: How Do They Work?

airline.payrollmaster
Partial Listing

```
proc sql;
    select EmpID, LastName,
       FirstName, City, State
    from airline.staffmaster
    where EmpID in
       (select EmpID
        from airline.payrollmaster
        where month(DateOfBirth)=2);
```

EmpID	DateOfBirth
. . .	. . .
1038	11/13/1967
1420	02/23/1963
1561	12/03/1961
1434	07/14/1960
1414	03/28/1970
1112	12/03/1962
1390	02/23/1963
1332	09/20/1968
. . .	. . .

Virtual table contains '1420','1390','1403','1404','1834','1103'.

93

c2s6d02

Noncorrelated Subqueries: How Do They Work?

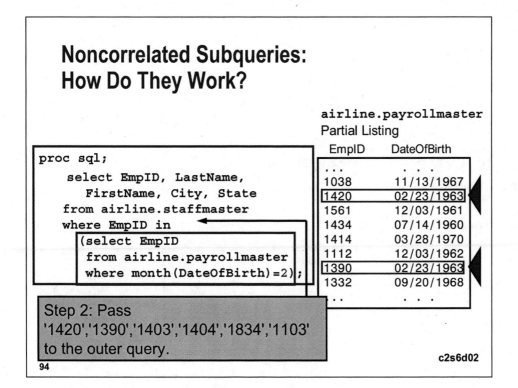

airline.payrollmaster
Partial Listing

EmpID	DateOfBirth
...	. . .
1038	11/13/1967
1420	02/23/1963
1561	12/03/1961
1434	07/14/1960
1414	03/28/1970
1112	12/03/1962
1390	02/23/1963
1332	09/20/1968
. .	. . .

```
proc sql;
    select EmpID, LastName,
        FirstName, City, State
    from airline.staffmaster
    where EmpID in
        (select EmpID
         from airline.payrollmaster
         where month(DateOfBirth)=2);
```

Step 2: Pass
'1420','1390','1403','1404','1834','1103'
to the outer query.

94

c2s6d02

Noncorrelated Subqueries: Output

The SAS System

Emp ID	LastName	FirstName	City	State
1403	BOWDEN	EARL	BRIDGEPORT	CT
1404	CARTER	DONALD	NEW YORK	NY
1834	LONG	RUSSELL	NEW YORK	NY
1103	MCDANIEL	RONDA	NEW YORK	NY
1420	ROUSE	JEREMY	PATERSON	NJ
1390	SMART	JONATHAN	NEW YORK	NY

Does this look familiar?

95

Selecting Data

If you specify the ANY keyword before a subquery, the comparison is true if it is true for any of the values that the subquery returns.

Keyword ANY	Signifies...
> ANY(20,30,40) returned from inner query	>20
< ANY(20,30,40) returned from inner query	< 40
= ANY(20,30,40) returned from inner query	=20 or =30 or =40

96

The ANY Keyword

Example: Are any low-level flight attendants (FA1 or FA2) older than any of the high-level flight attendants (FA3)?

> Think
> `<select max(DateOfBirth)`

```
proc sql;
title "FA1's or FA2's Older Than ANY FA3's";
   select EmpID, JobCode, DateOfBirth
      from airline.payrollmaster
      where JobCode in ('FA1','FA2')
        and DateOfBirth < any
           (select DateOfBirth
                from airline.payrollmaster
                where JobCode='FA3');
```

alternate   Select max(DOB) . . .

97   c2s6d03

This would be equivalent to asking, "Who is older than any single level-3 flight attendant?" An alternative WHERE clause is

```
where JobCode in ('FA1','FA2') and DateOfBirth <
   (select max(DateOfBirth) from...);
```

The ANY Keyword

Partial Output

```
      FA1's or FA2's Older Than ANY FA3's

      Emp    Job
      ID     Code   DateOfBirth
      _____

      1574   FA2    01MAY1958
      1475   FA2    19DEC1959
      1124   FA1    14JUL1956
      1422   FA1    08JUN1962
      1368   FA2    15JUN1959
      1411   FA2    31MAY1959
      1477   FA2    25MAR1962
      1970   FA1    29SEP1962
      1413   FA2    20SEP1963
      1434   FA2    15JUL1960
      1390   FA2    23FEB1963
```

98

The ALL Keyword

The ALL keyword is true only if the comparison is true for all values returned.

Keyword ALL	Signifies...
> ALL(20,30,40) returned from inner query	> 40
< ALL(20,30,40) returned from inner query	< 20

99

Selecting Data

Example: Are there FA1's or FA2's who are older than all
of the FA3's?

```
Think
<select min(DateOfBirth)
```

```
proc sql;
title "FA1's or FA2's Older Than ALL
FA3's";
    select EmpID, JobCode, DateOfBirth
        from airline.payrollmaster
        where JobCode in('FA1','FA2')
            and DateOfBirth < all
                (select DateOfBirth
                from airline.payrollmaster
                where JobCode='FA3');
```

alternate   select min(DOB)...   (More efficient)

.c2s6d04

100

An alternative WHERE clause is

```
where JobCode in('FA1','FA2') and DateOfBirth <
    (select min(DateOfBirth) from ...);
```

Selecting Data

Output

```
        FA1's or FA2's Older Than ALL FA3's

        Emp   Job
        ID    Code  DateOfBirth
        ─────────────────────────────
        1124  FA1      13JUL1956
        1415  FA2      12MAR1956
```

101

Correlated Subqueries

Rules for correlated subqueries include the following:

- cannot be evaluated independently, but depend on the values returned by the outer query for their results
- are evaluated for each row in the outer query

102

Correlated Subqueries

Example: Display the names and states of all navigator managers.

```
proc sql;
    select LastName, FirstName, State
        from airline.staffmaster
        where 'NA'=
            (select JobCategory
                from airline.supervisors
                where staffmaster.EmpID=
                      supervisors.EmpID) ;
```

You must qualify each column with a table name.

(handwritten notes:) Where empid in (Select empid from airline.sup where sup. empid = 'NA') jobcat-

c2s6d05

103

What does it mean to *qualify* a column? When a column appears in more than one table, the column name is preceded with the table name or alias to avoid ambiguity. In this example you use the table names **staffmaster** and **supervisors** in front of the column name of **EmpID**. Although table aliases are not used in this example, they are merely table nicknames and are discussed further in Section 3.2.

Correlated Subqueries

airline.staffmaster
Partial Listing

EmpID	LastName	FirstName
➤ 1919	ADAMS	GERALD
1401	AVERY	JERRY
1269	CASTON	FRANKLIN
1935	FERNANDEZ	KATRINA
1124	FIELDS	DIANA
1677	KRAMER	JACKSON
1442	NEWKIRK	SANDRA
1417	NEWKIRK	WILLIAM
1352	RIVERS	SIMON

airline.supervisors
Partial Listing

EmpID	State	JobCategory
1677	CT	BC
1834	NY	BC
1431	CT	FA
1433	NJ	FA
1385	CT	ME
1420	NJ	ME
1882	NY	ME
1935	CT	NA
1417	NJ	NA
1352	NY	NA
1106	CT	PT
1442	NJ	PT
1405	NJ	SC
1564	NY	SC
1401	NJ	TA

```
proc sql;
   select LastName, FirstName, State
      from airline.staffmaster
      where 'NA'=
         (select JobCategory
          from airline.supervisors
      where staffmaster.EmpID=
          supervisors.EmpID);
```

Step 1: The outer query takes the first row in **airline.staffmaster** and finds the **EmpID**, **LastName**, **FirstName**, and **State**.

104

Correlated Subqueries

airline.staffmaster
Partial Listing

EmpID	LastName	FirstName
➤ 1919	ADAMS	GERALD
1401	AVERY	JERRY
1269	CASTON	FRANKLIN
1935	FERNANDEZ	KATRINA
1124	FIELDS	DIANA
1677	KRAMER	JACKSON
1442	NEWKIRK	SANDRA
1417	NEWKIRK	WILLIAM
1352	RIVERS	SIMON

airline.supervisors
Partial Listing

EmpID	State	JobCategory
1677	CT	BC
1834	NY	BC
1431	CT	FA
1433	NJ	FA
1385	CT	ME
1420	NJ	ME
1882	NY	ME
1935	CT	NA
1417	NJ	NA
1352	NY	NA
1106	CT	PT
1442	NJ	PT
1405	NJ	SC
1564	NY	SC
1401	NJ	TA
		...

```
proc sql;
   select LastName, FirstName, State
      from airline.staffmaster
      where 'NA'=
         (select JobCategory
          from airline.supervisors
      where staffmaster.EmpID=
          supervisors.EmpID);
```

Step 2: Match **staffmaster.EmpID** with **supervisors.EmpID** to find the qualifying row in **airline.supervisors**.

airline.staffmaster.EmpID=
airline.supervisors.EmpID?

NO MATCH

105

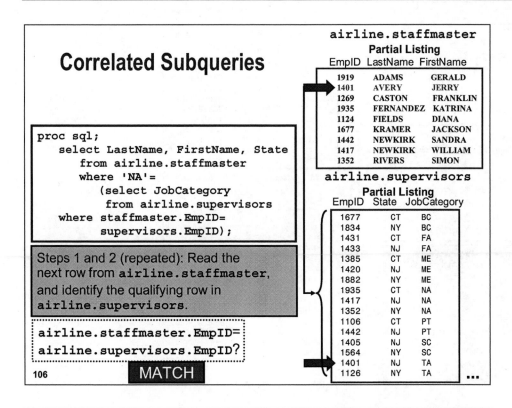

Correlated Subqueries

```
proc sql;
   select LastName, FirstName, State
      from airline.staffmaster
      where 'NA'=
         (select JobCategory
          from airline.supervisors
   where staffmaster.EmpID=
         supervisors.EmpID);
```

Steps 1 and 2 (repeated): Read the next row from `airline.staffmaster`, and identify the qualifying row in `airline.supervisors`.

`airline.staffmaster.EmpID=`
`airline.supervisors.EmpID?`

MATCH

106

airline.staffmaster
Partial Listing

EmpID	LastName	FirstName
1919	ADAMS	GERALD
1401	AVERY	JERRY
1269	CASTON	FRANKLIN
1935	FERNANDEZ	KATRINA
1124	FIELDS	DIANA
1677	KRAMER	JACKSON
1442	NEWKIRK	SANDRA
1417	NEWKIRK	WILLIAM
1352	RIVERS	SIMON

airline.supervisors
Partial Listing

EmpID	State	JobCategory
1677	CT	BC
1834	NY	BC
1431	CT	FA
1433	NJ	FA
1385	CT	ME
1420	NJ	ME
1882	NY	ME
1935	CT	NA
1417	NJ	NA
1352	NY	NA
1106	CT	PT
1442	NJ	PT
1405	NJ	SC
1564	NY	SC
1401	NJ	TA
1126	NY	TA

...

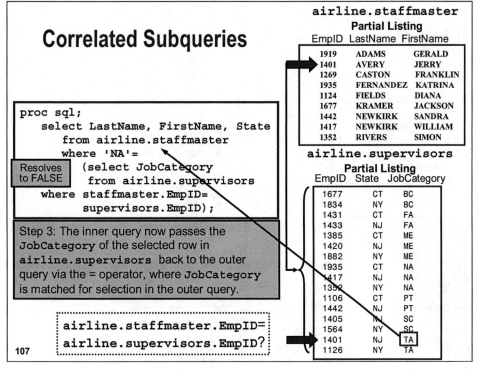

Correlated Subqueries

```
proc sql;
   select LastName, FirstName, State
      from airline.staffmaster
      where 'NA'=
         (select JobCategory
          from airline.supervisors
   where staffmaster.EmpID=
         supervisors.EmpID);
```

Resolves to FALSE

Step 3: The inner query now passes the `JobCategory` of the selected row in `airline.supervisors` back to the outer query via the = operator, where `JobCategory` is matched for selection in the outer query.

`airline.staffmaster.EmpID=`
`airline.supervisors.EmpID?`

107

airline.staffmaster
Partial Listing

EmpID	LastName	FirstName
1919	ADAMS	GERALD
1401	AVERY	JERRY
1269	CASTON	FRANKLIN
1935	FERNANDEZ	KATRINA
1124	FIELDS	DIANA
1677	KRAMER	JACKSON
1442	NEWKIRK	SANDRA
1417	NEWKIRK	WILLIAM
1352	RIVERS	SIMON

airline.supervisors
Partial Listing

EmpID	State	JobCategory
1677	CT	BC
1834	NY	BC
1431	CT	FA
1433	NJ	FA
1385	CT	ME
1420	NJ	ME
1882	NY	ME
1935	CT	NA
1417	NJ	NA
1352	NY	NA
1106	CT	PT
1442	NJ	PT
1405	NJ	SC
1564	NY	SC
1401	NJ	TA
1126	NY	TA

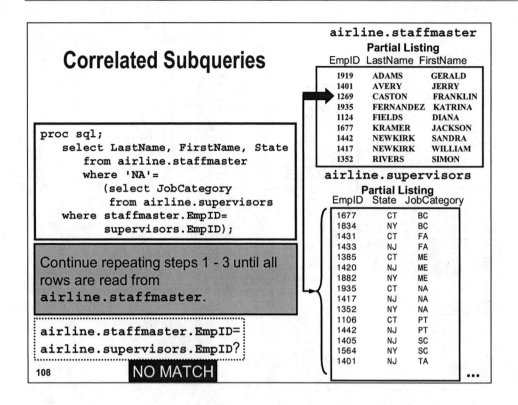

Correlated Subqueries

airline.staffmaster
Partial Listing

EmpID	LastName	FirstName
1919	ADAMS	GERALD
1401	AVERY	JERRY
1269	CASTON	FRANKLIN
1935	FERNANDEZ	KATRINA
1124	FIELDS	DIANA
1677	KRAMER	JACKSON
1442	NEWKIRK	SANDRA
1417	NEWKIRK	WILLIAM
1352	RIVERS	SIMON

```
proc sql;
   select LastName, FirstName, State
     from airline.staffmaster
     where 'NA'=
       (select JobCategory
         from airline.supervisors
   where staffmaster.EmpID=
     supervisors.EmpID);
```

Continue repeating steps 1 - 3 until all rows are read from `airline.staffmaster`.

`airline.staffmaster.EmpID=`
`airline.supervisors.EmpID?`

108   NO MATCH

airline.supervisors
Partial Listing

EmpID	State	JobCategory
1677	CT	BC
1834	NY	BC
1431	CT	FA
1433	NJ	FA
1385	CT	ME
1420	NJ	ME
1882	NY	ME
1935	CT	NA
1417	NJ	NA
1352	NY	NA
1106	CT	PT
1442	NJ	PT
1405	NJ	SC
1564	NY	SC
1401	NJ	TA

...

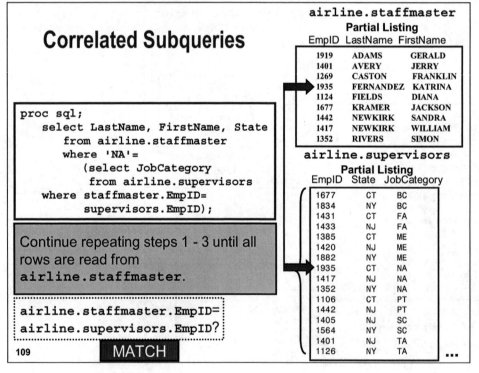

Correlated Subqueries

airline.staffmaster
Partial Listing

EmpID	LastName	FirstName
1919	ADAMS	GERALD
1401	AVERY	JERRY
1269	CASTON	FRANKLIN
1935	FERNANDEZ	KATRINA
1124	FIELDS	DIANA
1677	KRAMER	JACKSON
1442	NEWKIRK	SANDRA
1417	NEWKIRK	WILLIAM
1352	RIVERS	SIMON

```
proc sql;
   select LastName, FirstName, State
     from airline.staffmaster
     where 'NA'=
       (select JobCategory
         from airline.supervisors
   where staffmaster.EmpID=
     supervisors.EmpID);
```

Continue repeating steps 1 - 3 until all rows are read from `airline.staffmaster`.

`airline.staffmaster.EmpID=`
`airline.supervisors.EmpID?`

109   MATCH

airline.supervisors
Partial Listing

EmpID	State	JobCategory
1677	CT	BC
1834	NY	BC
1431	CT	FA
1433	NJ	FA
1385	CT	ME
1420	NJ	ME
1882	NY	ME
1935	CT	NA
1417	NJ	NA
1352	NY	NA
1106	CT	PT
1442	NJ	PT
1405	NJ	SC
1564	NY	SC
1401	NJ	TA
1126	NY	TA

...

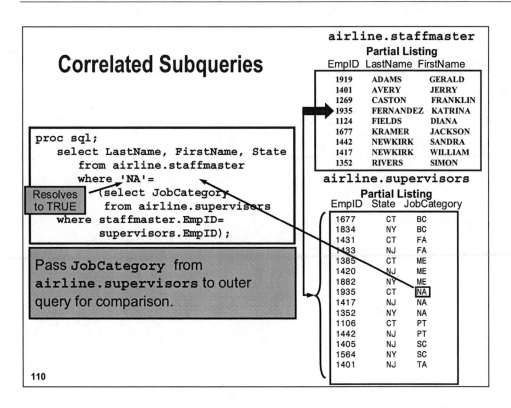

Correlated Subqueries

airline.staffmaster
Partial Listing

EmpID	LastName	FirstName
1919	ADAMS	GERALD
1401	AVERY	JERRY
1269	CASTON	FRANKLIN
1935	FERNANDEZ	KATRINA
1124	FIELDS	DIANA
1677	KRAMER	JACKSON
1442	NEWKIRK	SANDRA
1417	NEWKIRK	WILLIAM
1352	RIVERS	SIMON

airline.supervisors
Partial Listing

EmpID	State	JobCategory
1677	CT	BC
1834	NY	BC
1431	CT	FA
1433	NJ	FA
1385	CT	ME
1420	NJ	ME
1882	NY	ME
1935	CT	NA
1417	NJ	NA
1352	NY	NA
1106	CT	PT
1442	NJ	PT
1405	NJ	SC
1564	NY	SC
1401	NJ	TA

```
proc sql;
   select LastName, FirstName, State
      from airline.staffmaster
      where 'NA'=
         (select JobCategory
          from airline.supervisors
       where staffmaster.EmpID=
          supervisors.EmpID);
```

Resolves to TRUE

Pass **JobCategory** from **airline.supervisors** to outer query for comparison.

110

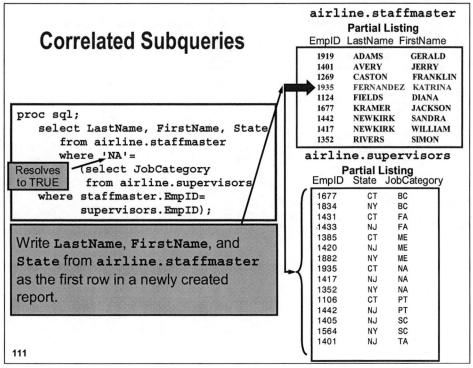

Correlated Subqueries

airline.staffmaster
Partial Listing

EmpID	LastName	FirstName
1919	ADAMS	GERALD
1401	AVERY	JERRY
1269	CASTON	FRANKLIN
1935	FERNANDEZ	KATRINA
1124	FIELDS	DIANA
1677	KRAMER	JACKSON
1442	NEWKIRK	SANDRA
1417	NEWKIRK	WILLIAM
1352	RIVERS	SIMON

airline.supervisors
Partial Listing

EmpID	State	JobCategory
1677	CT	BC
1834	NY	BC
1431	CT	FA
1433	NJ	FA
1385	CT	ME
1420	NJ	ME
1882	NY	ME
1935	CT	NA
1417	NJ	NA
1352	NY	NA
1106	CT	PT
1442	NJ	PT
1405	NJ	SC
1564	NY	SC
1401	NJ	TA

```
proc sql;
   select LastName, FirstName, State
      from airline.staffmaster
      where 'NA'=
         (select JobCategory
          from airline.supervisors
       where staffmaster.EmpID=
          supervisors.EmpID);
```

Resolves to TRUE

Write **LastName**, **FirstName**, and **State** from **airline.staffmaster** as the first row in a newly created report.

111

Correlated Subqueries

Build first row of report:

LastName	FirstName	State
FERNANDEZ	KATRINA	CT

112

SAS continues this process until all rows are read from the table referred to in the outer query, `airline.staffmaster`. At that point the third and final row of the report is written, as noted in the following slide.

Correlated Subqueries

Build third (and final) row of report:

LastName	FirstName	State
FERNANDEZ	KATRINA	CT
NEWKIRK	WILLIAM	NJ
RIVERS	SIMON	NY

125

Correlated Subqueries

The EXISTS condition tests for the existence of a set of values returned by the subquery.

- The EXISTS condition is true if the subquery returns at least one row.
- The NOT EXISTS condition is true if the subquery returns no data.

126

Correlated Subqueries

Example: The temporary table **work.fa** is a subset of **airline.staffmaster** containing the names and IDs of all flight attendants.

The **airline.flightschedule** table contains a row for each crew member assigned to a flight for each date.

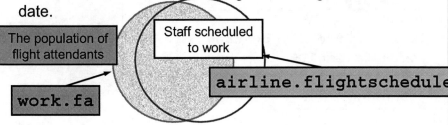

The population of flight attendants

work.fa

Staff scheduled to work

airline.flightschedule

127

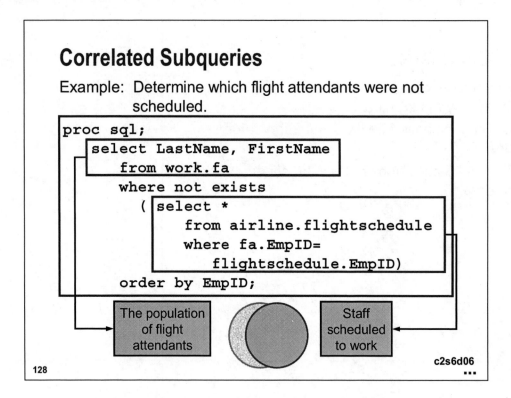

Correlated Subqueries

Example: Determine which flight attendants were not
scheduled.

```
proc sql;
   select LastName, FirstName
      from work.fa
      where not exists
         ( select *
            from airline.flightschedule
            where fa.EmpID=
               flightschedule.EmpID)
      order by EmpID;
```

The population of flight attendants

Staff scheduled to work

128

c2s6d06

...

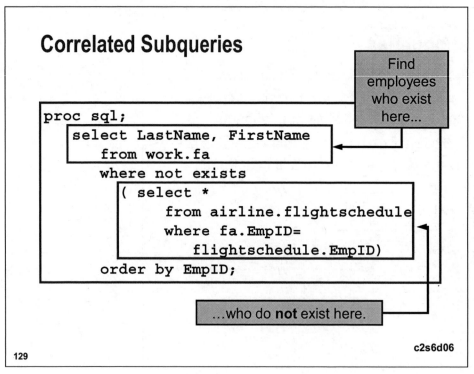

Correlated Subqueries

Find employees who exist here...

```
proc sql;
   select LastName, FirstName
      from work.fa
      where not exists
         ( select *
            from airline.flightschedule
            where fa.EmpID=
               flightschedule.EmpID)
      order by EmpID;
```

...who do **not** exist here.

129

c2s6d06

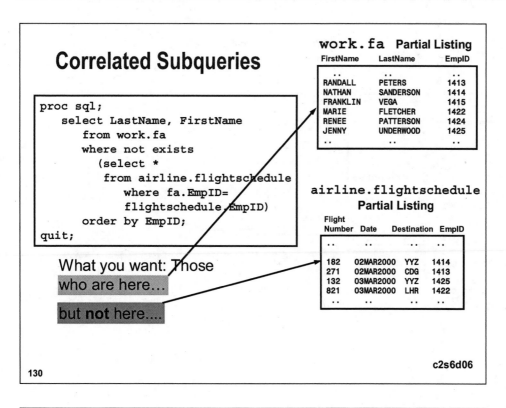

Correlated Subqueries

```
proc sql;
    select LastName, FirstName
        from work.fa
        where not exists
          (select *
          from airline.flightschedule
              where fa.EmpID=
              flightschedule.EmpID)
        order by EmpID;
quit;
```

What you want: Those
who are here...

but **not** here....

work.fa Partial Listing

FirstName	LastName	EmpID
..	..	..
RANDALL	PETERS	1413
NATHAN	SANDERSON	1414
FRANKLIN	VEGA	1415
MARIE	FLETCHER	1422
RENEE	PATTERSON	1424
JENNY	UNDERWOOD	1425
..	..	..

airline.flightschedule
Partial Listing

Flight Number	Date	Destination	EmpID
..	..	..	..
182	02MAR2000	YYZ	1414
271	02MAR2000	CDG	1413
132	03MAR2000	YYZ	1425
821	03MAR2000	LHR	1422
..	..	..	..

c2s6d06

130

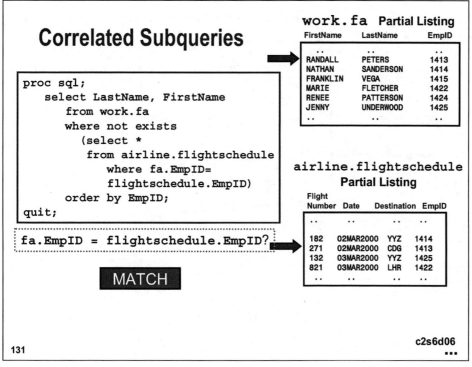

Correlated Subqueries

```
proc sql;
    select LastName, FirstName
        from work.fa
        where not exists
          (select *
          from airline.flightschedule
              where fa.EmpID=
              flightschedule.EmpID)
        order by EmpID;
quit;
```

`fa.EmpID = flightschedule.EmpID?`

MATCH

work.fa Partial Listing

FirstName	LastName	EmpID
..	..	..
RANDALL	PETERS	1413
NATHAN	SANDERSON	1414
FRANKLIN	VEGA	1415
MARIE	FLETCHER	1422
RENEE	PATTERSON	1424
JENNY	UNDERWOOD	1425
..	..	..

airline.flightschedule
Partial Listing

Flight Number	Date	Destination	EmpID
..	..	..	..
182	02MAR2000	YYZ	1414
271	02MAR2000	CDG	1413
132	03MAR2000	YYZ	1425
821	03MAR2000	LHR	1422
..	..	..	..

c2s6d06

131

...

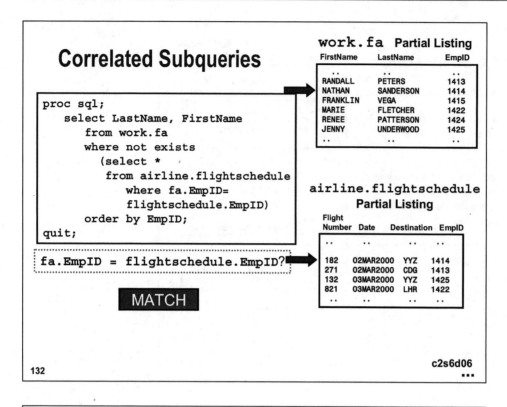

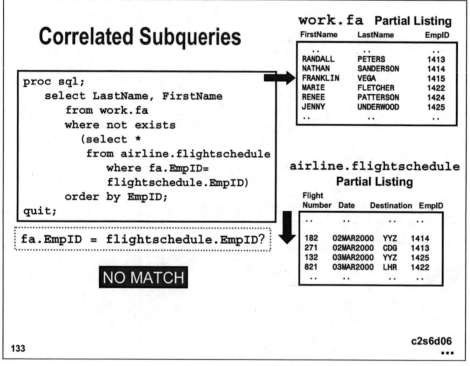

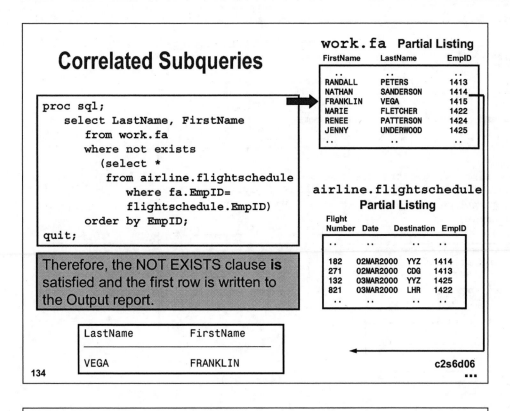

Correlated Subqueries

```
proc sql;
   select LastName, FirstName
      from work.fa
      where not exists
        (select *
         from airline.flightschedule
            where fa.EmpID=
            flightschedule.EmpID)
         order by EmpID;
quit;
```

Therefore, the NOT EXISTS clause **is** satisfied and the first row is written to the Output report.

LastName	FirstName
VEGA	FRANKLIN

work.fa Partial Listing

FirstName	LastName	EmpID
..	..	..
RANDALL	PETERS	1413
NATHAN	SANDERSON	1414
FRANKLIN	VEGA	1415
MARIE	FLETCHER	1422
RENEE	PATTERSON	1424
JENNY	UNDERWOOD	1425
..	..	..

airline.flightschedule Partial Listing

Flight Number	Date	Destination	EmpID
..	..	..	..
182	02MAR2000	YYZ	1414
271	02MAR2000	CDG	1413
132	03MAR2000	YYZ	1425
821	03MAR2000	LHR	1422
..	..	..	..

134   c2s6d06
                                         ...

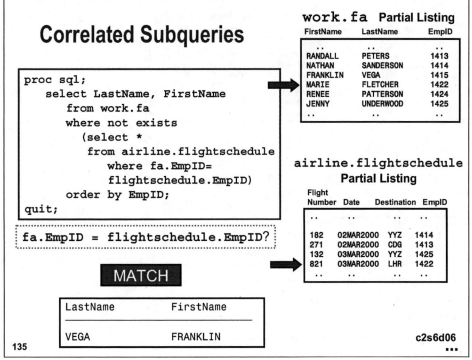

Correlated Subqueries

```
proc sql;
   select LastName, FirstName
      from work.fa
      where not exists
        (select *
         from airline.flightschedule
            where fa.EmpID=
            flightschedule.EmpID)
         order by EmpID;
quit;
```

fa.EmpID = flightschedule.EmpID?

MATCH

LastName	FirstName
VEGA	FRANKLIN

work.fa Partial Listing

FirstName	LastName	EmpID
..	..	..
RANDALL	PETERS	1413
NATHAN	SANDERSON	1414
FRANKLIN	VEGA	1415
MARIE	FLETCHER	1422
RENEE	PATTERSON	1424
JENNY	UNDERWOOD	1425
..	..	..

airline.flightschedule Partial Listing

Flight Number	Date	Destination	EmpID
..	..	..	..
182	02MAR2000	YYZ	1414
271	02MAR2000	CDG	1413
132	03MAR2000	YYZ	1425
821	03MAR2000	LHR	1422
..	..	..	..

135   c2s6d06
                                         ...

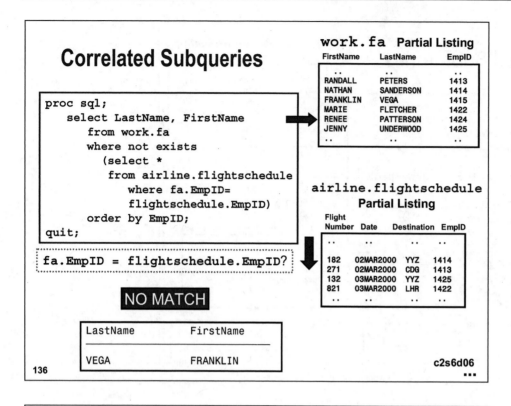

Correlated Subqueries

work.fa Partial Listing

FirstName	LastName	EmpID
..	..	..
RANDALL	PETERS	1413
NATHAN	SANDERSON	1414
FRANKLIN	VEGA	1415
MARIE	FLETCHER	1422
RENEE	PATTERSON	1424
JENNY	UNDERWOOD	1425
..	..	..

```
proc sql;
   select LastName, FirstName
      from work.fa
      where not exists
        (select *
         from airline.flightschedule
            where fa.EmpID=
            flightschedule.EmpID)
      order by EmpID;
quit;
```

`fa.EmpID = flightschedule.EmpID?`

airline.flightschedule
Partial Listing

Flight Number	Date	Destination	EmpID
..	..	..	..
182	02MAR2000	YYZ	1414
271	02MAR2000	CDG	1413
132	03MAR2000	YYZ	1425
821	03MAR2000	LHR	1422
..	..	..	..

NO MATCH

LastName	FirstName
VEGA	FRANKLIN

136   c2s6d06
                                                                          ...

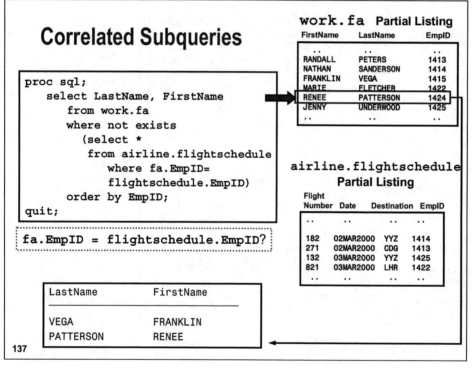

Correlated Subqueries

work.fa Partial Listing

FirstName	LastName	EmpID
..	..	..
RANDALL	PETERS	1413
NATHAN	SANDERSON	1414
FRANKLIN	VEGA	1415
MARIE	FLETCHER	1422
RENEE	PATTERSON	1424
JENNY	UNDERWOOD	1425
..	..	..

```
proc sql;
   select LastName, FirstName
      from work.fa
      where not exists
        (select *
         from airline.flightschedule
            where fa.EmpID=
            flightschedule.EmpID)
      order by EmpID;
quit;
```

`fa.EmpID = flightschedule.EmpID?`

airline.flightschedule
Partial Listing

Flight Number	Date	Destination	EmpID
..	..	..	..
182	02MAR2000	YYZ	1414
271	02MAR2000	CDG	1413
132	03MAR2000	YYZ	1425
821	03MAR2000	LHR	1422
..	..	..	..

LastName	FirstName
VEGA	FRANKLIN
PATTERSON	RENEE

137

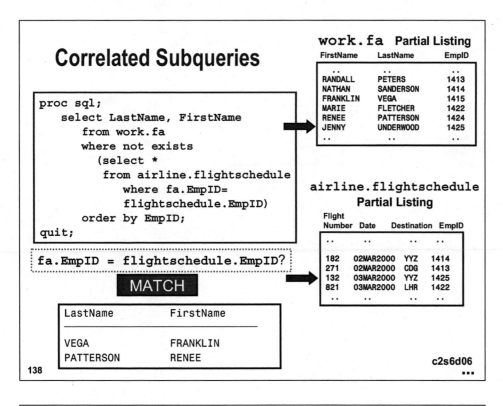

Correlated Subqueries

```
proc sql;
   select LastName, FirstName
      from work.fa
      where not exists
        (select *
         from airline.flightschedule
            where fa.EmpID=
            flightschedule.EmpID)
        order by EmpID;
quit;
```

work.fa Partial Listing

FirstName	LastName	EmpID
..	..	..
RANDALL	PETERS	1413
NATHAN	SANDERSON	1414
FRANKLIN	VEGA	1415
MARIE	FLETCHER	1422
RENEE	PATTERSON	1424
JENNY	UNDERWOOD	1425
..	..	..

fa.EmpID = flightschedule.EmpID?

MATCH

airline.flightschedule
Partial Listing

Flight Number	Date	Destination	EmpID
..	..	..	..
182	02MAR2000	YYZ	1414
271	02MAR2000	CDG	1413
132	03MAR2000	YYZ	1425
821	03MAR2000	LHR	1422
..	..	..	..

LastName	FirstName
VEGA	FRANKLIN
PATTERSON	RENEE

138

c2s6d06

...

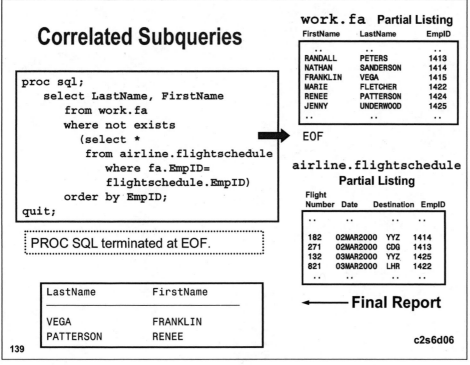

Correlated Subqueries

```
proc sql;
   select LastName, FirstName
      from work.fa
      where not exists
        (select *
         from airline.flightschedule
            where fa.EmpID=
            flightschedule.EmpID)
        order by EmpID;
quit;
```

work.fa Partial Listing

FirstName	LastName	EmpID
..	..	..
RANDALL	PETERS	1413
NATHAN	SANDERSON	1414
FRANKLIN	VEGA	1415
MARIE	FLETCHER	1422
RENEE	PATTERSON	1424
JENNY	UNDERWOOD	1425
..	..	..

EOF

airline.flightschedule
Partial Listing

Flight Number	Date	Destination	EmpID
..	..	..	..
182	02MAR2000	YYZ	1414
271	02MAR2000	CDG	1413
132	03MAR2000	YYZ	1425
821	03MAR2000	LHR	1422
..	..	..	..

PROC SQL terminated at EOF.

← Final Report

LastName	FirstName
VEGA	FRANKLIN
PATTERSON	RENEE

139

c2s6d06

Correlated Subqueries

Final Report

LastName	FirstName
PATTERSON	RENEE
VEGA	FRANKLIN

140

 **Exercises**

Submit a LIBNAME statement to assign the libref **airline** to the course SAS data library.
(TSO only: DISP=SHR)

TSO: `libname airline '.sql.sasdata';`

Directory-based systems: `libname airline '.';`

6. **Summarizing Data**

   Use the **airline.flightdelays** table to answer the questions.

   a. What was the maximum delay experienced for any flight in the table?

   b. What was the maximum delay experienced by each of the destinations?

   c. What was the average delay for each destination?

   d. Which destinations have an average delay that is greater than the overall average delay?

   Hint: Use a subquery to calculate the overall average delay.

7. **Summarizing Data in Groups**

   Use the **airline.staffmaster** table to determine the number of people employed by the airline
   in each city. Order the report by state and city.

   Output

   ```
              Number of Employees in Each City


                                        Number
             State  City               Employed
            ─────────────────────────────────────
             CT     BRIDGEPORT              19
             CT     STAMFORD                25
             NJ     PATERSON                 5
             NJ     PRINCETON               10
             NY     MT. VERNON               5
             NY     NEW YORK                79
             NY     WHITE PLAINS             5
   ```

8. Subqueries

Each month a memo is posted that lists the employees who have employment anniversaries for that month. Create the report for February and list the first and last names of all employees who were hired during the month of February of any year. You can find employee names in the **airline.staffmaster** table, and employee hire dates in the **airline.payrollmaster** table. Order the report by employee last name.

Output

```
              Employees with February Anniversaries

                  FirstName        LastName
                  _____   _____

                  JUSTIN           BLAIR
                  JASON            BROWN
                  GERALD           FOSTER
                  MICHAEL          HOWARD
                  MARILYN          REED
                  WAYNE            THOMPSON
                  KATHY            TRIPP
                  FRANKLIN         VEGA
                  CHIN             WANG
                  ELAINE           WARD
                  CAROLYN          WHALEY
```

9. Correlated Subqueries (Optional)

Create a report that shows the number of employees who are frequent flyers of the airline. Employees are listed in **airline.staffmaster** and frequent flyers are in **airline.frequentflyers**. (Hint: Names are stored differently in the two tables.)

Output

```
              Number of Employees Listed
                 in Frequent Flyer Table

                        count
                        _____

                         136
```

10. Summarizing Data (Optional)

a. Use the **airline.flightdelays** table to determine the number of times each flight was delayed. (Hint: There should be one row for each flight.) Order the report by flight number.

Partial Output

Delayed Arrivals		
FlightNumber	Destination	Times Delayed
114	LAX	19
132	YYZ	21
182	YYZ	15
183	WAS	16
202	ORD	16

b. Use the **airline.flightdelays** table to determine the number of times each flight was on time (Times Delayed=0). Order your report by flight number.

Partial Output

On-Time Arrivals		
FlightNumber	Destination	On-time Count
114	LAX	3
132	YYZ	2
182	YYZ	3
183	WAS	3
202	ORD	2

2.7 Chapter Summary

The SQL procedure enables you to use SQL statements in a SAS program. When you use the SQL procedure, you do not need to repeat the PROC SQL statement with each query, and you do not need a RUN statement. Results of the query are displayed automatically and can be ordered. Queries contain statements that are composed of clauses.

A SELECT statement is used to query one or more SAS data sets. Use the SELECT statement to retrieve data from a table and to specify how to display a report.

You can use the VALIDATE keyword to verify the validity of the query's syntax. Messages are printed in the SAS log.

You can calculate new columns by using expressions or DATA step functions. You can subset rows by using a WHERE clause or eliminate duplicate rows by using the DISTINCT keyword. The CALCULATED keyword enables you to use a previously calculated value elsewhere in the query. Use a GROUP BY clause to apply summary functions to groups of values and include an ORDER BY clause to sort the output. You can customize output with SAS formats, labels, and titles.

Summary functions are available to summarize data for the entire table or for groups of data in the table. You can select groups of data to be processed by using a HAVING clause.

You can use a subquery to select data from a table based on the result returned by another query. Subqueries are typically used in a WHERE or HAVING clause and are evaluated before the outer query. A correlated subquery is a subquery that depends on values returned by the outer query.

General form of the SELECT statement:

```
SELECT column-1<, column-2> ...
     FROM table-1|view-1<, table-2|view-2> ...
     <WHERE expression>
     <GROUP BY column-1<, column-2> ...>
     <HAVING expression>
     <ORDER BY column-1<, column-2> ... <DESC>>;
```

2.8 Solutions to Exercises

1. **Querying a Table**

a.

```
proc sql;
   select *
      from airline.payrollmaster;
```

b.

```
select EmpID, Gender, JobCode, Salary
   from airline.payrollmaster;
```

c.

```
select EmpID, Gender, JobCode, Salary,
       Salary/3 as Tax
   from airline.payrollmaster;
```

d.

```
select EmpID, Gender, JobCode,
       Salary format=comma10.2,
       Salary/3 as Tax format=comma10.2
   from airline.payrollmaster;
```

e.

```
select EmpID, Gender, JobCode,
       Salary format=comma10.2,
       Salary/3 as Tax format=comma10.2
   from airline.payrollmaster
   where Gender='M';
```

f.

```
select EmpID, Gender, JobCode,
       Salary format=comma10.2,
       Salary/3 as Tax format=comma10.2
   from airline.payrollmaster
   where Gender='M' and JobCode contains 'FA';
quit;
```

2. **Eliminating Duplicates**

```
proc sql;
title 'Cities Where Employees Live';
   select distinct City
      from airline.staffmaster
      order by City;
quit;
title;
```

3. Subsetting Data

```
proc sql;
title 'Flights Less Than One Third Full';
    select FlightNumber, Date, Destination,
            Boarded+Transferred+Nonrevenue as Total,
            PassengerCapacity
    from airline.marchflights
    where calculated Total<(PassengerCapacity/3)
    order by 4 desc;
quit;
title;
```

4. Querying Data (Optional)

```
proc sql;
title "Frequent Fliers with First Names Beginning with an 'N'";
    select Name, ffid
        from airline.frequentflyers
        where Name like '%, N%';
quit;
title;
```

Alternate Solution

```
select Name, ffid
    from airline.frequentflyers
    where left(scan(Name,2,',')) like 'N%';
```

5. Using SAS Functions (Optional)

```
proc sql;
title 'Employee Age Information';
    select EmpID label='Employee ID',
            DateOfBirth format=mmddyy10.
                label='Birth Date',
            DateOfHire format=mmddyy10.
                label='Hire Date',
            int((DateOfHire-DateOfBirth)/365.25)
                label='Age At Employment'
        from airline.payrollmaster;
quit;
title;
```

6. Summarizing Data

a.

```
proc sql;
title 'Maximum Delay Experienced';
    select max(Delay) label='Max Delay'
        from airline.flightdelays;
```

b.

```
title 'Maximum Delay Experienced';
title2 'by Each Destination';
   select Destination,
          max(Delay) label='Max Delay'
      from airline.flightdelays
      group by Destination;
```

c.

```
title 'Average Delay for Each Destination';
   select Destination,
          avg(Delay) label='Average Delay'
      from airline.flightdelays
      group by Destination;
```

d.

```
title 'Destinations Having Average Delay';
title2 'Exceeding Overall Average';
   select Destination,
          avg(Delay) label='Average Delay'
      from airline.flightdelays
      group by Destination
      having avg(Delay) >
         (select avg(Delay)
            from airline.flightdelays);
quit;
title;
```

7. Summarizing Data in Groups

```
proc sql;
title 'Number of Employees in Each City';
   select State, City,
          count(*) label='Number Employed'
      from airline.staffmaster
      group by State, City
      order by State, City;
quit;
title;
```

8. Subqueries

```
proc sql;
title 'Employees with February Anniversaries';
   select FirstName, LastName
      from airline.staffmaster
      where EmpID in
         (select EmpID
            from airline.payrollmaster
            where month(DateOfHire)=2);
quit;
title;
```

9.   Correlated Subqueries (Optional)

```
proc sql;
title 'Number of Employees Listed';
title2 'in Frequent Flyer Table';
   select count(*) as count
       from airline.frequentflyers
       where exists
          (select *
              from airline.staffmaster
              where Name=trim(LastName)||', '||FirstName);
quit;
title;
```

10.   Summarizing Data (Optional)

   a.

```
proc sql;
title 'Delayed Arrivals';
   select FlightNumber, Destination,
          count(*) label='Times Delayed'
       from airline.flightdelays
       where Delay>0
       group by FlightNumber, Destination
       order by FlightNumber;
```

   b.

```
title 'On-time Arrivals';
   select FlightNumber, Destination,
          count(*) label='On-time Count'
       from airline.flightdelays
       where Delay=0
       group by FlightNumber, Destination
       order by FlightNumber;
quit;
title;
```

Chapter 3   Combining Tables

3.1 Overview

Objectives

- Distinguish between joins and set operations.

3

Combining Data from Multiple Tables

Joins combine tables horizontally (side by side).

Table A	Table B

4

Combining Data from Multiple Tables

Set operations combine tables vertically (one on top
of the other).

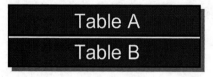

5

Which DATA step statements perform similar operations?

3.2 Joins

Objectives

- Describe the different joins available in PROC SQL.
- Use a table alias.
- Compare SQL joins to DATA step merges.

7

Types of Joins

PROC SQL supports the following two types of joins:

- inner joins
- outer joins

8

Types of Joins

Inner joins have the following characteristics:

- return only matching rows
- allow a maximum of 32 tables to be joined at the same time

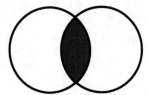

9

    If the join involves views, the number of tables underlying the views, not the views themselves, counts toward the limit of 32.

Outer Joins

You can retrieve nonmatching rows, as well as matching rows, by using an outer join. Outer joins are limited to two tables at a time.

Left   Full   Right

35

Cartesian Product

A query that lists multiple tables in the FROM clause, without row restrictions, results in all possible combinations of rows from all tables. This is called a *Cartesian product*.

```
select *
        from one, two;
```

c3s2d01

11

Cartesian Product

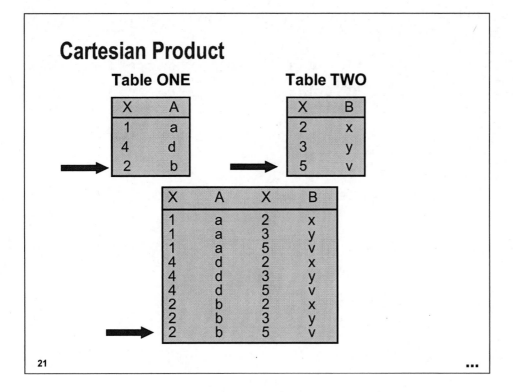

Table ONE

X	A
1	a
4	d
2	b

Table TWO

X	B
2	x
3	y
5	v

X	A	X	B
1	a	2	x
1	a	3	y
1	a	5	v
4	d	2	x
4	d	3	y
4	d	5	v
2	b	2	x
2	b	3	y
2	b	5	v

21

...

Cartesian Product

The number of rows in a Cartesian product is the product of the number of rows in the contributing tables.

$$3 \times 3 = 9$$

$$1,000 \times 1,000 = 1,000,000$$

22   ...

 A Cartesian product is rarely a desired query outcome. The SQL processor prints a warning in the log if a query involved a Cartesian product:

NOTE: The execution of this query involves performing one or more Cartesian product joins that cannot be optimized.

Inner Joins

Inner join syntax resembles Cartesian product syntax, but it has a WHERE clause that restricts how the rows can be combined.

General form of an inner join:

> **SELECT** *column-1, column-2, …*
>   **FROM** *table-1, table-2, …*
>   **WHERE** *join-condition(s)*
>   **<AND** *other subsetting conditions>*
>   *<other clauses>;*

23

The distinguishing characteristics of inner join syntax are

- a list of two or more table names in the FROM clause
- one or more join conditions in the WHERE clause.

Inner Joins

Conceptually, PROC SQL performs the following tasks:
- first builds a Cartesian product
- then applies the specified restriction(s) and removes rows

24

Inner Joins

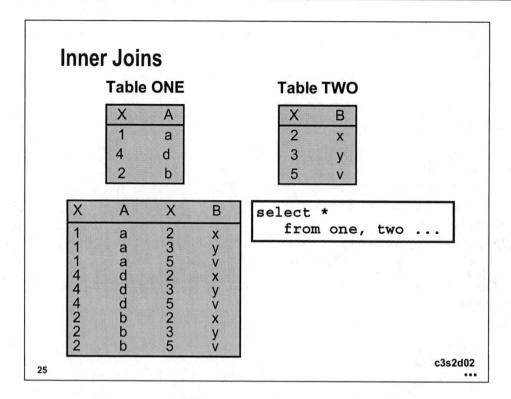

Inner Joins

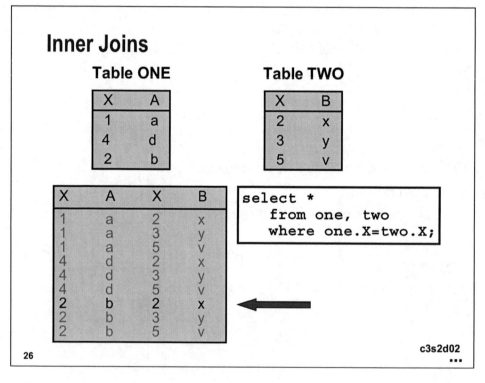

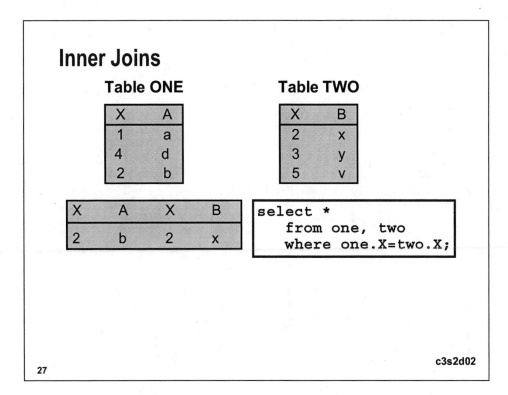

An inner join is sometimes called a conventional join, natural join, or *equijoin*.

Tables do not have to be sorted before they are joined.

Column X exists in both tables and occurs twice in the query result.

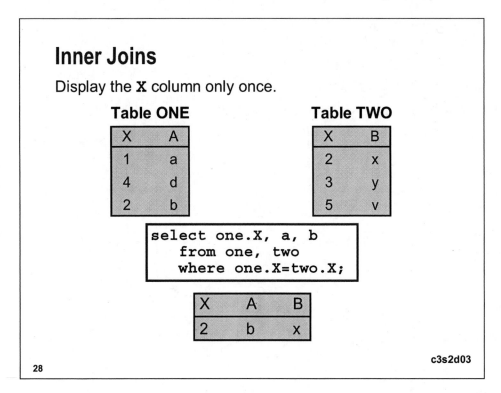

Inner Joins

Display all combinations of rows with matching keys, including duplicates.

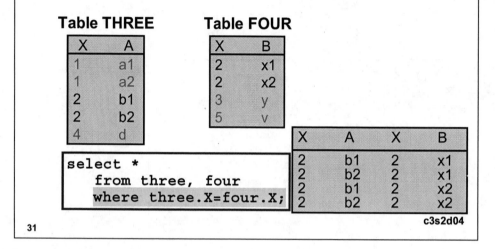

Table THREE

X	A
1	a1
1	a2
2	b1
2	b2
4	d

Table FOUR

X	B
2	x1
2	x2
3	y
5	v

X	A	X	B
2	b1	2	x1
2	b2	2	x1
2	b1	2	x2
2	b2	2	x2

```
select *
    from three, four
    where three.X=four.X;
```

31

c3s2d04

How many rows does a DATA step match-merge produce for X = 2?

Inner Joins

Example: Display the names, job codes, and ages of all New York employees.

- Employee names are found in the **airline.staffmaster** table.
- Employee job codes and birth dates are found in the **airline.payrollmaster** table.

32

Inner Joins

```
title 'New York Employees';
③select substr(FirstName,1,1)||'. ' ||
        LastName as Name,
        JobCode,
        int((today()-DateOfBirth)/365.25)
            as Age
①from airline.payrollmaster,
        airline.staffmaster
②where payrollmaster.EmpID=
        staffmaster.EmpID
        and State='NY'
    order by JobCode;
```

33

c3s2d05

Inner Joins

Partial Output (rows 49-58)

```
                    New York Employees

                                    Job
Name                                Code        Age
_____

J.  BOYCE                           PT1         43
R.  VENTER                          PT1         35
D.  CARTER                          PT2         55
J.  NEWTON                          PT2         49
L.  UPCHURCH                        PT2         53
W.  THOMPSON                        PT2         54
R.  STEPHENSON                      PT2         57
R.  LUFKIN                          PT3         56
R.  DENNIS                          PT3         64
J.  BRADLEY                         SCP         41
```

34

This program was run on September 12, 2006. Your results may differ.

Outer Joins

You can retrieve nonmatching rows, as well as matching rows, by using an outer join. Outer joins are limited to two tables at a time.

Left   Full   Right

35

 An outer join is an augmentation of an inner join. It returns all the rows generated by an inner join, plus others.

Outer Joins

General form of an outer join:

```
SELECT column <, column> ...
    FROM table1
        LEFT|RIGHT|FULL JOIN
            table2
        ON join-condition(s)
    <other clauses>;
```

36

The distinguishing characteristics of outer join syntax are

- exactly two table names flanking one of the three JOIN operators in the FROM clause
- a special ON clause specifying the join condition(s).

A WHERE clause is permitted in order to specify general subsetting conditions.

Outer Joins

A left join retrieves matching rows from both tables, plus nonmatching rows from the left table (the first table in the FROM clause).

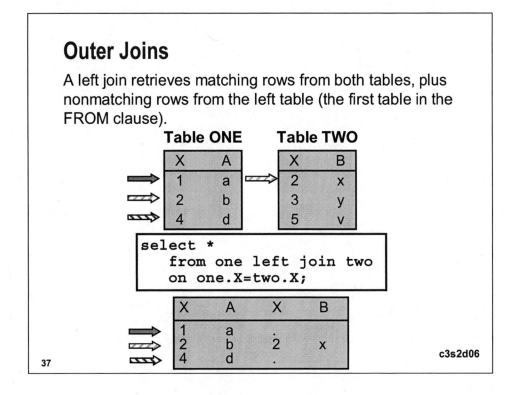

37

c3s2d06

Outer Joins

A right join retrieves matching rows from both tables, plus nonmatching rows from the right table (the second table in the FROM clause).

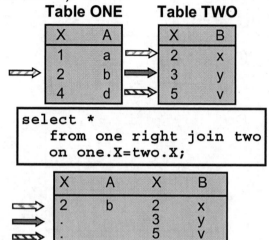

Table ONE

X	A
1	a
2	b
4	d

Table TWO

X	B
2	x
3	y
5	v

```
select *
    from one right join two
    on one.X=two.X;
```

X	A	X	B
2	b	2	x
.		3	y
.		5	v

38

c3s2d07

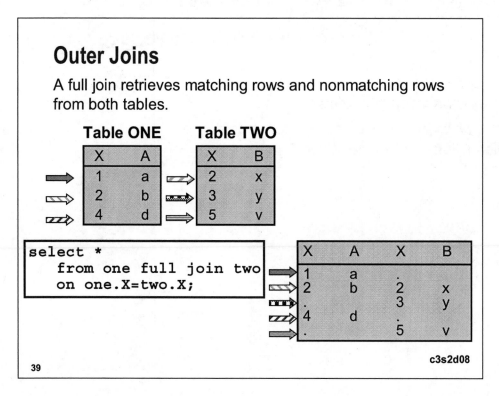

Outer Joins

A full join retrieves matching rows and nonmatching rows from both tables.

```
select *
   from one full join two
   on one.X=two.X;
```

39   c3s2d08

Compare this result with the Cartesian product demonstrated earlier.

You can also write an inner join using this style of syntax:

```
SELECT *
    FROM table-1
    INNER JOIN table-two
    ON table-1.x = table2.x;
```

but the join is limited to two tables.

Outer Joins

Example: List all flights during March with corresponding
delay information (if it exists).

✎ `airline.flightdelays` does not contain
delay information for all of the March flights.

40

Outer Joins

```
title 'All March Flights';
proc sql;
 (3)select marchflights.Date,
         marchflights.FlightNumber
             label='Flight Number',
         marchflights.Destination
             label='Left',
         flightdelays.Destination
             label='Right',
         Delay
 (1) from airline.marchflights
         left join
         airline.flightdelays
 (2) on marchflights.Date=flightdelays.Date
       and marchflights.FlightNumber=
           flightdelays.FlightNumber
     order by Delay;
```

41   c3s2d09

Outer Joins
Partial Output

	Flight			DelayIn
Date	Number	Left	Right	Minutes
16MAR2000	622	FRA		.
03MAR2000	416	WAS		.
17MAR2000	182	YYZ		.
14MAR2000	271	CDG		.
11MAR2000	290	WAS		.
08MAR2000	182	YYZ		.
.	132	YYZ		.
11MAR2000	202	ORD		.
29MAR2000	829	WAS		.
25MAR2000	872	LAX		.
22MAR2000	183	WAS		.
27MAR2000	982	DFW		.
25MAR2000	829	WAS	WAS	-10
18MAR2000	219	LHR	LHR	-10
09MAR2000	821	LHR	LHR	-10

All March Flights

42

Using a Table Alias

An *alias* is a table nickname. You can assign an alias to a table by following the table name in the FROM clause with the AS keyword and a nickname for the table. Then use the alias in other clauses of the QUERY statement.

43

A table alias is primarily used to reduce the amount of typing required to write a query. It is usually optional. There are, however, two situations that require a table alias:

- a self-join (a table is joined to itself), for example,

```
from airline.staffmaster as s1, airline.staffmaster as s2
```

- when referencing same-named columns from same-named tables in different libraries, for example,

```
from airline.flightdelays as ad,
   work.flightdelays as wd
      where ad.delay > wd.delay
```

Using a Table Alias

```
select l.Date,
       l.FlightNumber
          label='Flight Number',
       l.Destination label='Left',
       r.Destination label='Right',
       Delay
   from airline.marchflights as l
       left join
       airline.flightdelays as r
   on l.Date=r.Date and
      l.FlightNumber=r.FlightNumber
   order by Delay;
```

don't need 'as'

c3s2d10

44

The AS keyword is optional in a table alias. The alias can directly follow the table name in the FROM clause.

SQL Join versus DATA Step Merge

A DATA step with MERGE and BY statements combines rows differently from an outer join.

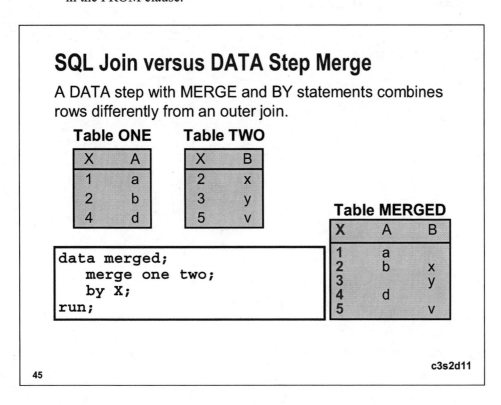

Table ONE

X	A
1	a
2	b
4	d

Table TWO

X	B
2	x
3	y
5	v

Table MERGED

X	A	B
1	a	
2	b	x
3		y
4	d	
5		v

```
data merged;
   merge one two;
   by X;
run;
```

c3s2d11

45

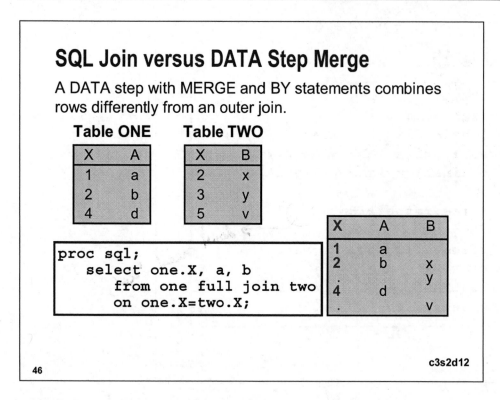

SQL Join versus DATA Step Merge

A DATA step with MERGE and BY statements combines rows differently from an outer join.

Table ONE

X	A
1	a
2	b
4	d

Table TWO

X	B
2	x
3	y
5	v

X	A	B
1	a	
2	b	x
.		y
4	d	
.		v

```
proc sql;
    select one.X, a, b
        from one full join two
        on one.X=two.X;
```

46

c3s2d12

In the SQL procedure, the two X columns are not overlaid by default.

How can you achieve the same result using PROC SQL?

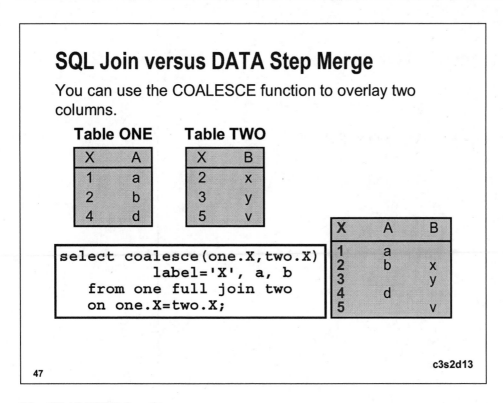

SQL Join versus DATA Step Merge

You can use the COALESCE function to overlay two columns.

Table ONE

X	A
1	a
2	b
4	d

Table TWO

X	B
2	x
3	y
5	v

```
select coalesce(one.X,two.X)
        label='X', a, b
  from one full join two
  on one.X=two.X;
```

X	A	B
1	a	
2	b	x
3		y
4	d	
5		v

47

c3s2d13

The COALESCE function

- returns the first value that is a SAS nonmissing value

- requires all arguments to have the same data type.

If you omit the LABEL= option or an alias in a coalesced column, it appears without a column heading.

🖉   If the tables being joined together had multiple matching keyfield values between the tables, the data step and the SQL procedure would not give the same results. SQL would be the only method that generates a Cartesian Product of all the matching rows

SQL Join versus DATA Step Merge

Joins do not require the following:

- sorted or indexed tables
- same-named columns in join expressions
- equality in join expressions

48

Tables can be joined on inequalities, for example,

```
select columns
   from table1 as a, table2 as b
   where  a.itemnumber=b.itemnumber
    and a.cost > b.price;
```

non-eq join
(Can't do this in data step)

Internal Processing of Joins

Conceptually, during a join, SQL performs the following tasks:

- a Cartesian product is built internally
- WHERE processing selects the appropriate rows

In reality, however, the PROC SQL optimizer breaks the Cartesian product into smaller pieces.

Algorithms
- *Sort*
- *Index*
- *Hash*
- *Brute force*

49

SAS data sets are stored in pages that contain a certain number of observations. To reduce input/output, the SQL procedure optimizer uses these pages in its processing.

During a two-way join, the following tasks are completed:

1. The first page from table A is read into memory, with as many of the first pages from table B that can fit into available memory.

2. Valid rows are selected.

3. The first page of table A is kept in memory. All subsequent pages from table B that can fit into memory are read and step 2 is repeated.

4. All pages from table B are processed in combination with page 1 from table A. Steps 1 through 4 are repeated for page 2 from table A. The entire process stops when all rows in both tables are processed.

The SQL procedure optimizer can process an equijoin (a join on an equals condition, for example, **where x.idnum=y.idnum**) more efficiently than a join involving an inequality.

During a two-way equijoin, the following tasks are completed:

1. Both tables are sorted by the matching column (if necessary) and are grouped by the matching column's value into chunks.

2. The Cartesian product is only performed on matching portions of data.

3. After a section of data is processed, it is not processed again.

> The SQL procedure optimizer has other algorithms from which to select when you optimize a join. For example, you can use a hashing algorithm when you join a small table with a large table.

In a multiway join (more than two tables), in order to minimize the Cartesian product, the SQL procedure optimizer

*   splits the join into a number of two-way joins, and eliminates rows and columns from the intermediate tables as soon as they are no longer required

*   decides the order in which the tables are processed

*   processes the joins in the order that minimizes the intermediate Cartesian product..

3.3 Complex Joins

Objectives

- Understand techniques that simplify the coding of a complex query.
- Compare solving a problem using PROC SQL with traditional SAS programming.

51

In-Line Views

An *in-line view* has the following characteristics:

- a temporary table that exists only during query execution
- created when a FROM clause contains a query expression in place of a table name

52

In-Line Views

Example: Which destinations experience the worst delays?

How do you define worst delays?

53

In-Line Views

Output

Destination	Average Delay	Maximum Delay	Number of Delays	Number of Early Arrivals	Probability of Delay
WAS	1	15	76	75	0.50
YYZ	2	14	36	24	0.60
DFW	3	20	38	23	0.62
ORD	3	19	51	41	0.55
LAX	5	27	82	41	0.67
LHR	6	30	39	19	0.67
CPH	6	26	16	11	0.59
FRA	6	34	14	12	0.54
CDG	9	39	21	5	0.81

54

In-Line Views

```
select Destination,
       summarized columns,
       late / (late + early) as prob
          format=5.2
          label='Probability of Delay'
    from summarized table
    order by 2nd column;
```

55

In-Line Views

Boolean expressions can be used in the SELECT clause.

```
select Delay,
       (Delay > 0) as Late
    from airline.flightdelays;
```

Partial Output

Delay	Late
0	0
8	1
-5	0
18	1

c3s3d01

56

A Boolean expression resolves either to 1 (true) or 0 (false).

In-Line Views

```
select *, Late/(Late+Early) as prob
       format=5.2 label='Probability of Delay'
   from (select Destination,
             avg(Delay) as average
          format=3.0 label='Average Delay',
             max(Delay) as max
          format=3.0 label='Maximum Delay',
             sum(Delay > 0) as late
          format=3.0 label='Number of Delays',
             sum(Delay <= 0) as early
          format=3.0
             label='Number of Early Arrivals'
          from airline.flightdelays
          group by 1)
order by 2;
```

57   c3s3d02

When it is summed, a Boolean expression displays the number of rows that are true. A missing value will force a Boolean expression to resolve to true. Use a WHERE clause to omit missing value from the summarization.

You can use the calculated columns LATE and EARLY in the SELECT list because the in-line view is evaluated first.

In-Line Views

Output

Destination	Average Delay	Maximum Delay	Number of Delays	Number of Early Arrivals	Probability of Delay
WAS	1	15	76	75	0.50
YYZ	2	14	36	24	0.60
DFW	3	20	38	23	0.62
ORD	3	19	51	41	0.55
LAX	5	27	82	41	0.67
LHR	6	30	39	19	0.67
CPH	6	26	16	11	0.59
FRA	6	34	14	12	0.54
CDG	9	39	21	5	0.81

58

Handling a Complex Query

What are the names of the supervisors for the crew on the flight to Copenhagen on March 4, 2000?

Step 1:   Identify the crew for the flight.

Step 2:   Find the states and job categories of the crew returned from the first query.

Step 3:   Find the employee numbers of the crew supervisors based on the states and job categories generated by the second query.

Step 4:   Find the names of the supervisors based on the employee numbers returned from the third query.

59   ...

Because this query involves four tables,

- `airline.flightschedule`
- `airline.staffmaster`
- `airline.payrollmaster`
- `airline.supervisors`

it may not be easy to code all at once. Split the query into small parts and test it each time that a new part is added.

The columns needed for this query are as follows:

- `EmpID`
- `FirstName`
- `LastName`
- `Date`
- `Destination`
- `JobCode`
- `JobCategory`
- `State`

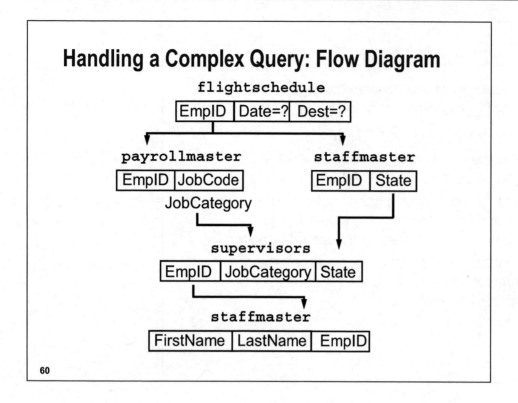

Handling a Complex Query: Flow Diagram

60

Handling a Complex Query

Step 1: Identify the crew for the flight.

```
select EmpID
    from airline.flightschedule
    where Date='04mar2000'd
          and Destination='CPH';
```

61   c3s3d03

Handling a Complex Query

Step 1: Output

Emp ID
1556
1830
1124
1135
1437
1839

62

Handling a Complex Query

Step 2:   Find the states and job categories of the crew
returned from the first query.

```
select substr(JobCode,1,2) as JobCategory,
       State
   from airline.staffmaster as s,
        airline.payrollmaster as p
   where s.EmpID=p.EmpID and s.EmpID in
       (select EmpID
          from airline.flightschedule
          where  Date='04mar2000'd
             and Destination='CPH');
```

list of 6 employees

63   c3s3d04

There is one supervisor for each state and job category.

Handling a Complex Query

Step 2: Output

JobCategory	State
FA	CT
FA	NY
NA	NY
PT	NY
PT	CT
FA	NY

64

Handling a Complex Query

Step 3: Find the employee numbers of the crew supervisors based on the states and job categories generated by the second query.

```
select EmpID
   from airline.supervisors as m,
      (select substr(JobCode,1,2) as JobCategory,
            State
         from airline.staffmaster as s,
            airline.payrollmaster as p
         where s.EmpID=p.EmpID and s.EmpID in
            (select EmpID
               from airline.flightschedule
               where Date='04mar2000'd and
                     Destination='CPH')) as c
   where  m.JobCategory=c.JobCategory
      and m.State=c.State;
```

in-line view

alias for in-line view

65   c3s3d05

✎   You can assign an alias to an in-line view.

Handling a Complex Query

Step 3: Output

Supervisor Id
1431
1983
1352
1118
1106
1983

66

✎   Note that ID number 1983 appears twice in the query result.

Handling a Complex Query

Step 4: Find the names of the supervisors.

```
select FirstName, LastName
   from airline.staffmaster where EmpID in
      (select EmpID
         from airline.supervisors as m,
            (select substr(JobCode,1,2) as
                  JobCategory, State
               from airline.staffmaster as s,
                  airline.payrollmaster as p
            where s.EmpID=p.EmpID and s.EmpID in
               (select EmpID
                  from airline.flightschedule
                  where Date='04mar2000'd and
                     Destination='CPH')) as c
   where  m.JobCategory=c.JobCategory
      and m.State=c.State);
```

c3s3d06

67

Handling a Complex Query

Step 4: Output

FirstName	LastName
SHARON	DEAN
ROGER	DENNIS
JASPER	MARSHBURN
SIMON	RIVERS
DEBORAH	YOUNG

68

Sharon Dean, ID 1983, appears once in this query result.

Handling a Complex Query

You can also solve this problem by using a multiway join.

```
select distinct e.FirstName, e.LastName
    from airline.flightschedule as a,
         airline.staffmaster as b,
         airline.payrollmaster as c,
         airline.supervisors as d,
         airline.staffmaster as e
   where a.Date='04mar2000'd and
         a.Destination='CPH' and
         a.EmpID=b.EmpID and
         a.EmpID=c.EmpID and
         d.JobCategory=substr(c.JobCode,1,2)
     and d.State=b.State and
         d.EmpID=e.EmpID;
```

69   c3s3d07

This code provides a more efficient solution to the query, but it is more difficult to build step-by-step.

You must have two copies of the **staffmaster** table: one to look up the states of the crew members and the other to look up the names of the supervisors. If you use a single copy of the table, it restricts the query to supervisors who were actually in the flight crew, if any.

Comparison with Traditional SAS Programs

Perform the same task using traditional SAS programming.

```
/* Find the crew for the flight. */
/* Program c3s3d08             */

proc sort data=airline.flightschedule (drop=flightnumber)
          out=crew (keep=empid);
   where destination='CPH' and date='04MAR2000'd;
   by empid;
run;


/* Find the State and job code for the crew. */

proc sort data=airline.payrollmaster (keep=empid jobcode)
          out=payroll;
   by empid;
run;


proc sort data=airline.staffmaster
              (keep=empid state firstname lastname)
          out=staff;
   by empid;
run;


data st_cat (keep=state jobcategory);
   merge crew (in=c)
         staff
         payroll;
   by empid;
   if c;
   jobcategory=substr(jobcode,1,2);
run;


/* Find the supervisor IDs. */

proc sort data=st_cat;
   by jobcategory state;
run;


proc sort data=airline.supervisors
          out=superv;
   by jobcategory state;
run;
```

(Continued on the next page.)

```
data super (keep=empid);
   merge st_cat(in=s)
         superv;
   by jobcategory state;
   if s;
run;

/* Find the names of the supervisors. */

proc sort data=super;
   by empid;
run;

data names(drop=empid);
   merge super (in=super)
         staff (keep=empid firstname lastname);
   by empid;
   if super;
run;

proc print data=names noobs uniform;
run;
```

Output

```
           LastName        FirstName

           MARSHBURN       JASPER
           DENNIS          ROGER
           RIVERS          SIMON
           YOUNG           DEBORAH
           DEAN            SHARON
           DEAN            SHARON
```

✎   The SQL query eliminated the duplicate names seen in this output.

In the example, the SQL query uses less CPU time, but more I/O operations than the non-SQL program (based on a mainframe benchmark in batch mode).

Choosing Between SQL Joins and DATA Step Merges

- DATA step merges are usually more efficient than SQL joins in combining small tables.
- SQL joins are usually more efficient than DATA step merges in combining large, unsorted tables.
- SQL joins are usually more efficient than DATA step merges in combining a large, indexed table with a small table.

70

A DATA step merge requires sorted data that calls for one or more SORT procedure steps. PROC SQL does not require sorted data.

Choosing Between SQL Joins and DATA Step Merges

- For ad hoc queries, select the method that you can code in the shortest time.
- For production jobs, experiment with different coding techniques and evaluate performance statistics.

71

 **Exercises**

Submit a LIBNAME statement to assign the libref **airline** to the course SAS data library:

TSO: `libname airline '.sql.sasdata';`

Directory-based systems: `libname airline '.';`

1. **Combining Data from Two Tables**

    Display the names of employees who have more than 20 years of service as of January 1, 2001. The **airline.staffmaster** table contains employee names, and the **airline.payrollmaster** table contains hire date information. Order the output by employee last name.

    ```
                Employees with > 20 Years of Service
                         as of 01JAN2001


              FirstName          LastName
              _____

              JOSEPH             BAREFOOT
              JUSTIN             BLAIR
              DAVIS              CARAWAY
              DONALD             CARTER
              ROGER              DENNIS
              KATRINA            FERNANDEZ
              RAYMOND            HARTFORD
              ANNE               KIRBY
              ROY                LUFKIN
              ALICE              MURPHY
              JAMES              PEARSON
              ROBERT             STEPHENSON
              WAYNE              THOMPSON
              ALAN               TUCKER
              THERESA            UPDIKE
              ELAINE             WARD
              DARIUS             WELCH
    ```

2. Combining Data from Two Tables

Enhance the output from Exercise **1** by showing the number of years of service for each employee as of January 1, 2001.

```
                    Employees with 20 Years of Service
                            as of 01JAN2001

                                              YearsOf
             FirstName        LastName         Service
             _____

             JOSEPH           BAREFOOT            22
             JUSTIN           BLAIR               21
             DAVIS            CARAWAY             24
             DONALD           CARTER              22
             ROGER            DENNIS              22
             KATRINA          FERNANDEZ           21
             RAYMOND          HARTFORD            21
             ANNE             KIRBY               22
             ROY              LUFKIN              21
             ALICE            MURPHY              22
             JAMES            PEARSON             22
             ROBERT           STEPHENSON          23
             WAYNE            THOMPSON            23
             ALAN             TUCKER              24
             THERESA          UPDIKE              21
             ELAINE           WARD                22
             DARIUS           WELCH               21
```

3. Combining Data from Two Tables

Create a report that compares the number of passengers boarded with the capacity of the flight for all international flights. The **airline.internationalflights** table contains boarding information for **international** flights, and the **airline.marchflights** table contains capacity information for **all** flights. Order the output by flight number and date.

Hints:

- Use the PERCENT5. format for the column calculated as **Boarded/PassengerCapacity**.

- Ignore the Boarded column in **airline.marchflights**.

Partial Output

```
                    Capacity Figures for International Flights

                                                 Passenger
          FlightNumber        Date   Boarded      Capacity   Percent

          132                    .        98           178      55%
          132            01MAR2000       115           178      65%
          132            02MAR2000       106           178      60%
          132            03MAR2000        75           178      42%
          132            04MAR2000       117           178      66%
          132            05MAR2000       157           178      88%
          132            06MAR2000       150           178      84%
          132            07MAR2000       164           178      92%
          132            08MAR2000       104           178      58%
          132            09MAR2000       119           178      67%
          132            10MAR2000        98           178      55%
```

4. Summarizing Data from Two Tables

Report the number of employees per job code for each state. Also display the average, maximum, and minimum salaries within the job code for each state. The **airline.staffmaster** table contains state data, and the **airline.payrollmaster** table contains job code and salary data. Order the report by state and job code.

Partial Output

State	Job Code	Total Employees	Average Salary	Maximum Salary	Minimum Salary
			Salary Statistics by State and Job Code		
CT	BCK	2	$36,038.80	$36,409.80	$35,667.80
CT	FA1	3	$32,615.80	$33,570.60	$31,175.20
CT	FA2	4	$39,373.25	$40,070.80	$38,498.60
CT	FA3	2	$46,433.80	$46,522.00	$46,345.60
CT	ME1	2	$39,121.60	$39,300.80	$38,942.40
CT	ME2	5	$49,864.08	$51,367.40	$49,151.20
CT	ME3	3	$59,600.33	$61,460.00	$58,171.40
CT	NA1	3	$58,866.27	$59,183.60	$58,366.00
CT	NA2	1	$71,513.40	$71,513.40	$71,513.40
CT	PT1	3	$95,962.07	$99,030.40	$92,582.00
CT	PT2	4	$121,587.90	$125,484.80	$118,259.40
CT	TA1	4	$38,736.25	$39,981.20	$37,146.20
CT	TA2	6	$47,056.80	$48,724.20	$45,887.80
CT	TA3	2	$55,638.10	$56,364.00	$54,912.20

5. Combining Data from Multiple Tables (Optional)

Create a flight and employee schedule that is ordered by flight number, date, last name, and first name. The data is in the tables **airline.staffmaster** (name information), **airline.flightschedule** (schedule information), and **airline.marchflights** (flight information).

Partial Output

Flt Num	Date	FirstName	LastName	Emp Num	Dep Time	Dest
		Flight Schedule for Airline Employees				
132	01MAR2000	JONATHAN	BOYCE	1739	15:35	YYZ
132	01MAR2000	SHARON	DEAN	1983	15:35	YYZ
132	01MAR2000	JAMES	NEWTON	1478	15:35	YYZ
132	01MAR2000	JEREMY	RHODES	1111	15:35	YYZ
132	01MAR2000	JONATHAN	SMART	1390	15:35	YYZ
132	01MAR2000	DEBORAH	WOOD	1130	15:35	YYZ
132	02MAR2000	MARSHALL	CAHILL	1574	15:35	YYZ
132	02MAR2000	JACKSON	JOHNSON	1411	15:35	YYZ
132	02MAR2000	LESLIE	JONES	1113	15:35	YYZ
132	02MAR2000	JAMES	NEWTON	1478	15:35	YYZ
132	02MAR2000	MICHAEL	PENNINGTON	1556	15:35	YYZ
132	02MAR2000	JEREMY	RHODES	1111	15:35	YYZ
132	03MAR2000	JONATHAN	BOYCE	1739	15:35	YYZ
132	03MAR2000	DOROTHY	CARTER	1437	15:35	YYZ
132	03MAR2000	JEREMY	RHODES	1111	15:35	YYZ

6. Combining Data from Multiple Tables (Optional)

Display the flight attendants (job code of FA_) who are scheduled to fly to Copenhagen (CPH). Gather information from the tables **airline.staffmaster** (name information), **airline.payrollmaster** (job code information), **and airline.flightschedule** (schedule information). Order the report by employee last name.

```
            Flight Attendants Scheduled for Copenhagen

                FirstName           LastName
                _____

                BARBARA             ARTHUR
                DOROTHY             CARTER
                ANTHONY             COOPER
                ALICIA              EATON
                DIANA               FIELDS
                MARIE               FLETCHER
                LESLIE              JONES
                KATHY               LAWRENCE
                CAROL               PEARCE
                EDITH               SANDERSON
                JONATHAN            SMART
                JENNY               UNDERWOOD
                ANNA                VEGA
                DIANE               WALTERS
                DEBORAH             WOOD
                DEBORAH             YOUNG
```

3.4 Set Operators

Objectives

- Use the SQL set operators.
- Compare the SQL set operators to traditional SAS programming tools.

74

Types of Set Operators

Set operators combine rows from two tables vertically.

The following are the four set operators:

- EXCEPT
- INTERSECT
- UNION
- OUTER UNION

General form of the set operators:

```
SELECT  column <, column> ... FROM table1
    set-operator <modifiers>
SELECT column <, column> ...  FROM table2 ;
```

75

Default Behavior of Set Operators

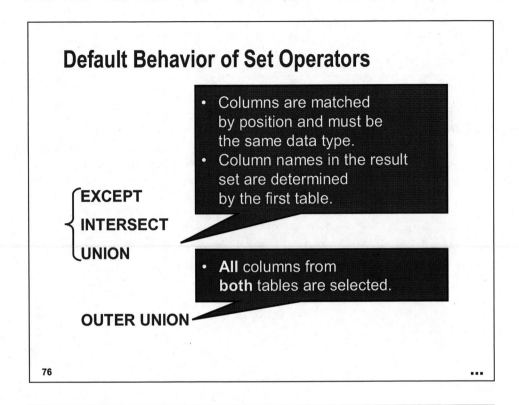

EXCEPT
INTERSECT
UNION

- Columns are matched by position and must be the same data type.
- Column names in the result set are determined by the first table.

OUTER UNION

- **All** columns from **both** tables are selected.

76   ...

Types of Set Operators

EXCEPT

- Unique rows from the first table that are not found in the second table are selected.

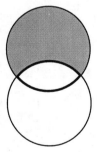

77

Types of Set Operators

INTERSECT

- Common unique rows from both
  tables are selected.

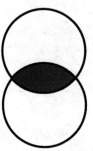

78

Types of Set Operators

UNION

- All unique rows from both tables
  are selected with columns
  overlaid.

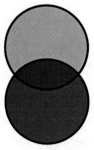

79

Types of Set Operators

OUTER UNION

- All rows from both tables, unique as well as non-unique, are selected.
- Columns are not overlaid.

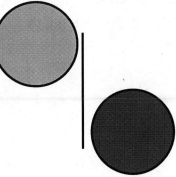

80

Modifiers

You can use the following two keywords to modify the behavior of set operators:

- ALL
- CORRESPONDING

81

Modifiers

The following are characteristics of the ALL keyword:

- does not remove duplicate rows, and so avoids an extra pass through the data. Use the ALL keyword for better performance when it is possible.

- is not allowed in connection with an OUTER UNION operator. (It is implicit.)

82

Use the ALL keyword when

- you do not care if there are duplicates
- duplicates are not possible; for example, there is a unique or primary key constraint on the column.

Modifiers

The following are characteristics of the CORRESPONDING keyword:

- overlays columns by name, instead of by position
- removes any columns not found in both tables when used in EXCEPT, INTERSECT, and UNION operations
- causes common columns to be overlaid when used in OUTER UNION operations
- can be abbreviated as CORR

83

Set Operators and Modifiers: Flow Diagram

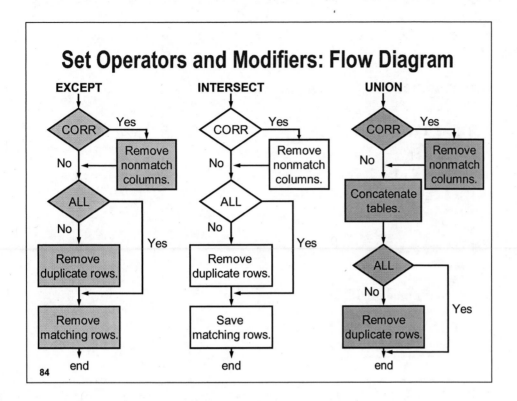

EXCEPT

CORR — Yes → Remove nonmatch columns.

No ↓

ALL — Yes →

No ↓

Remove duplicate rows.

↓

Remove matching rows.

↓

end

84

INTERSECT

CORR — Yes → Remove nonmatch columns.

No ↓

ALL — Yes →

No ↓

Remove duplicate rows.

↓

Save matching rows.

↓

end

UNION

CORR — Yes → Remove nonmatch columns.

No ↓

Concatenate tables.

↓

ALL — Yes →

No ↓

Remove duplicate rows.

↓

end

EXCEPT

- Unique rows from the first table that are not found in the second table are selected.

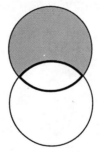

85

The EXCEPT Operator

Display the unique rows in table ONE that are not found in table TWO.

Table ONE

X	A
1	a
1	a
1	b
2	c
3	v
4	e
6	g

Table TWO

X	B
1	x
2	y
3	z
3	v
5	w

```
select *
    from one
except
select *
    from two;
```

86

c3s4d01

The EXCEPT Operator

The SQL processor removes duplicate rows within the tables.

Table ONE

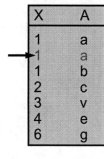

X	A
1	a
1	a
1	b
2	c
3	v
4	e
6	g

Table TWO

X	B
1	x
2	y
3	z
3	v
5	w

```
select *
    from one
except
select *
    from two;
```

87

c3s4d01

The EXCEPT Operator

The SQL processor creates an intermediate result set by returning the rows that are found only in table ONE.

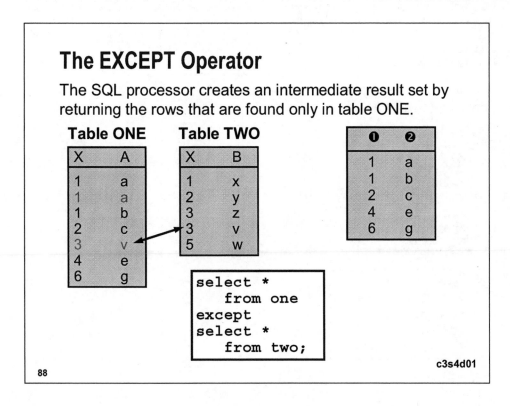

```
select *
    from one
except
select *
    from two;
```

c3s4d01

88

The EXCEPT Operator

The column names are determined by table ONE in the final result set.

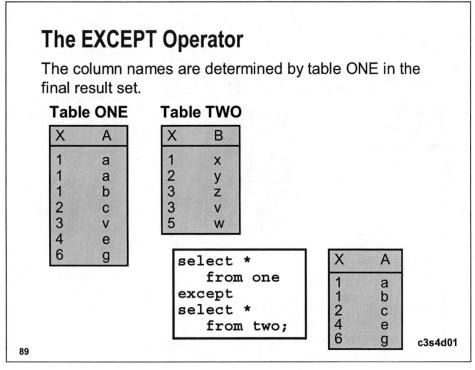

```
select *
    from one
except
select *
    from two;
```

c3s4d01

89

Duplicate rows are omitted.

How can you include duplicate rows?

The EXCEPT Operator

Display the rows (duplicates included) that are found in table ONE but not in table TWO.

Table ONE

X	A
1	a
1	a
1	b
2	c
3	v
4	e
6	g

Table TWO

X	B
1	x
2	y
3	z
3	v
5	w

```
select *
    from one
except all
select *
    from two;
```

90   c3s4d02

The EXCEPT Operator

The SQL processor creates an intermediate result set by returning the rows that are found only in table ONE.

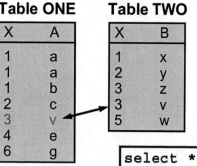

Table ONE

X	A
1	a
1	a
1	b
2	c
3	v
4	e
6	g

Table TWO

X	B
1	x
2	y
3	z
3	v
5	w

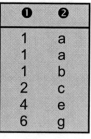

❶	❷
1	a
1	a
1	b
2	c
4	e
6	g

```
select *
    from one
except all
select *
    from two;
```

91   c3s4d02

The EXCEPT Operator

The column names are determined by table ONE in the final result set.

Table ONE

X	A
1	a
1	a
1	b
2	c
3	v
4	e
6	g

Table TWO

X	B
1	x
2	y
3	z
3	v
5	w

```
select *
    from one
except all
select *
    from two;
```

X	A
1	a
1	a
1	b
2	c
4	e
6	g

c3s4d02

92

The EXCEPT Operator

Display the unique rows that exist in table ONE and not in table TWO, based on same-named columns.

Table ONE

X	A
1	a
1	a
1	b
2	c
3	v
4	e
6	g

Table TWO

X	B
1	x
2	y
3	z
3	v
5	w

```
select *
    from one
except corr
select *
    from two;
```

c3s4d03

93

The EXCEPT Operator

The SQL processor eliminates any columns not found in both tables.

Table ONE

X	A
1	a
1	a
1	b
2	c
3	v
4	e
6	g

Table TWO

X	B
1	x
2	y
3	z
3	v
5	w

```
select *
    from one
except corr
select *
    from two;
```

94   c3s4d03

The EXCEPT Operator

Duplicate rows within each table are eliminated.

Table ONE

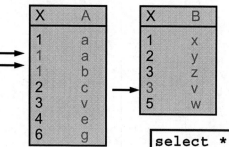

X	A
1	a
1	a
1	b
2	c
3	v
4	e
6	g

Table TWO

X	B
1	x
2	y
3	z
3	v
5	w

```
select *
    from one
except corr
select *
    from two;
```

95   c3s4d03

The EXCEPT Operator

The SQL processor creates an intermediate result set by returning the rows that are found only in table ONE.

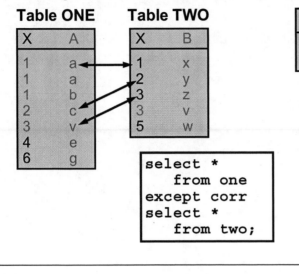

Table ONE

X	A
1	a
1	a
1	b
2	c
3	v
4	e
6	g

Table TWO

X	B
1	x
2	y
3	z
3	v
5	w

❶
4
6

```
select *
    from one
except corr
select *
    from two;
```

c3s4d03

96

The EXCEPT Operator

Final result set.

Table ONE

X	A
1	a
1	a
1	b
2	c
3	v
4	e
6	g

Table TWO

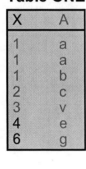

X	B
1	x
2	y
3	z
3	v
5	w

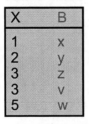

```
select *
    from one
except corr
select *
    from two;
```

X
4
6

c3s4d03

97

The EXCEPT Operator

`airline.staffchanges` and
`airline.payrollchanges` contain information
about

- current employees who have salary or job code changes
- new employees.

The new tables have the same layout as the
`airline.staffmaster` and
`airline.payrollmaster` tables.

98

The EXCEPT Operator

Example: Display the names of new employees.

```
select FirstName, LastName
   from airline.staffchanges
      except all
select FirstName, LastName
   from airline.staffmaster;
```

99

c3s4d04

The EXCEPT Operator

Output

FirstName	LastName
AMY	BRIDESTON
JIM	POWELL

100

The EXCEPT Operator

Example: How many employees have no changes in
salary or job code?

```
select count(*) label='No. of Persons'
   from (select EmpID
            from airline.staffmaster
         except all
         select EmpID
            from airline.staffchanges);
```

c3s4d05

101

The EXCEPT Operator

Output

No. of Persons
144

102

INTERSECT

- Common unique rows from both tables are selected.

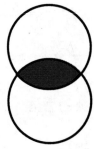

103

The INTERSECT Operator

Display the unique rows common to table ONE and table TWO.

Table ONE

X	A
1	a
1	a
1	b
2	c
3	v
4	e
6	g

Table TWO

X	B
1	x
2	y
3	z
3	v
5	w

```
select *
   from one
intersect
select *
   from two;
```

104   c3s4d06

The INTERSECT Operator

The SQL processor removes duplicate rows within the tables.

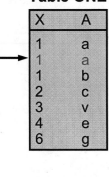

Table ONE

X	A
1	a
1	a
1	b
2	c
3	v
4	e
6	g

Table TWO

X	B
1	x
2	y
3	z
3	v
5	w

```
select *
   from one
intersect
select *
   from two;
```

105   c3s4d06

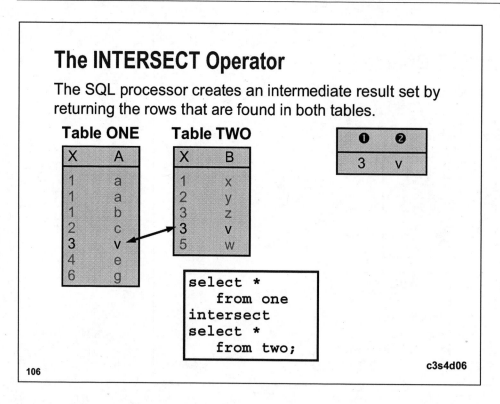

The INTERSECT Operator

The SQL processor creates an intermediate result set by returning the rows that are found in both tables.

Table ONE

X	A
1	a
1	a
1	b
2	c
3	v
4	e
6	g

Table TWO

X	B
1	x
2	y
3	z
3	v
5	w

❶	❷
3	v

```
select *
    from one
intersect
select *
    from two;
```

106   c3s4d06

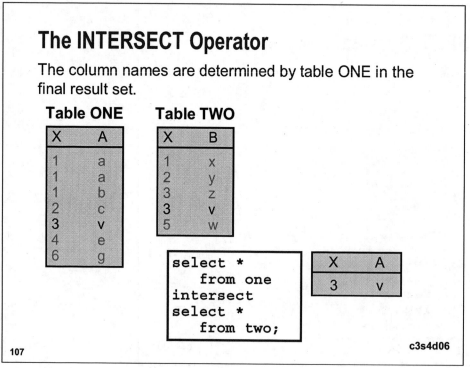

The INTERSECT Operator

The column names are determined by table ONE in the final result set.

Table ONE

X	A
1	a
1	a
1	b
2	c
3	v
4	e
6	g

Table TWO

X	B
1	x
2	y
3	z
3	v
5	w

```
select *
    from one
intersect
select *
    from two;
```

X	A
3	v

107   c3s4d06

Would the addition of the ALL keyword have any effect in this example?

The INTERSECT Operator

Display the unique rows common to table ONE and table TWO, based on same-named columns.

Table ONE

X	A
1	a
1	a
1	b
2	c
3	v
4	e
6	g

Table TWO

X	B
1	x
2	y
3	z
3	v
5	w

```
select *
    from one
intersect corr
select *
    from two;
```

→ ensures comparing cols with same names.

c3s4d07

108

The INTERSECT Operator

Duplicate rows within each table are eliminated.

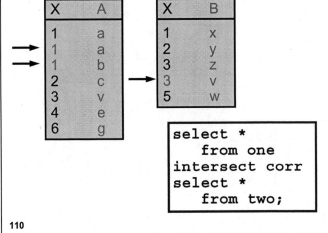

Table ONE

X	A
1	a
1	a
1	b
2	c
3	v
4	e
6	g

Table TWO

X	B
1	x
2	y
3	z
3	v
5	w

```
select *
    from one
intersect corr
select *
    from two;
```

c3s4d07

110

The INTERSECT Operator

The SQL processor creates an intermediate result set by returning the rows that are found in both tables.

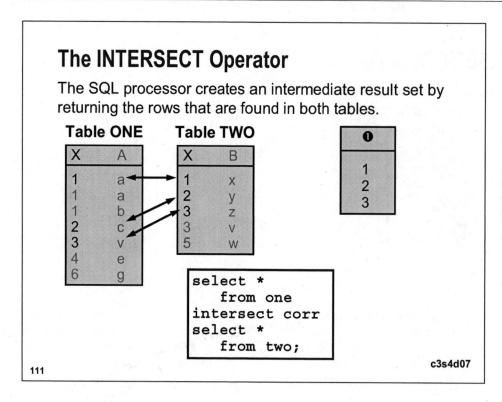

```
select *
    from one
intersect corr
select *
    from two;
```

111   c3s4d07

The INTERSECT Operator

Final result set.

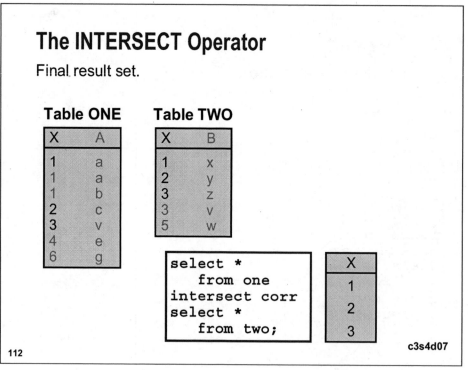

```
select *
    from one
intersect corr
select *
    from two;
```

112   c3s4d07

The INTERSECT Operator

Example: What are the names of the old employees who
changed salary or job code?

```
select FirstName, LastName
    from airline.staffmaster
        intersect all
select FirstName, LastName
    from airline.staffchanges;
```

*No need for corr
since col names
explicitly used in
SELECT statement*

c3s4d08

113

The INTERSECT Operator

Output

FirstName	LastName
DIANE	WALTERS
KAREN	CARTER
NEIL	CHAPMAN
RAYMOND	SANDERS

114

UNION

- All unique rows from both tables are selected with columns overlaid.

115

The UNION Operator

Display the unique rows that table ONE and table TWO have all together.

Table ONE

X	A
1	a
1	a
1	b
2	c
3	v
4	e
6	g

Table TWO

X	B
1	x
2	y
3	z
3	v
5	w

```
select *
    from one
union
select *
    from two;
```

116

c3s4d09

The UNION Operator

The SQL processor creates an intermediate result by concatenating and sorting ONE and TWO.

Table ONE

X	A
1	a
1	a
1	b
2	c
3	v
4	e
6	g

Table TWO

X	B
1	x
2	y
3	z
3	v
5	w

```
select *
    from one
union
select *
    from two;
```

❶	❷
1	a
1	a
1	b
1	x
2	c
2	y
3	v
3	v
3	z
4	e
5	w
6	g

c3s4d09

117

The UNION Operator

The SQL processor removes duplicate rows from the intermediate result.

Table ONE

X	A
1	a
1	a
1	b
2	c
3	v
4	e
6	g

Table TWO

X	B
1	x
2	y
3	z
3	v
5	w

```
select *
    from one
union
select *
    from two;
```

❶	❷
1	a
1	a
1	b
1	x
2	c
2	y
3	v
3	v
3	z
4	e
5	w
6	g

c3s4d09

118

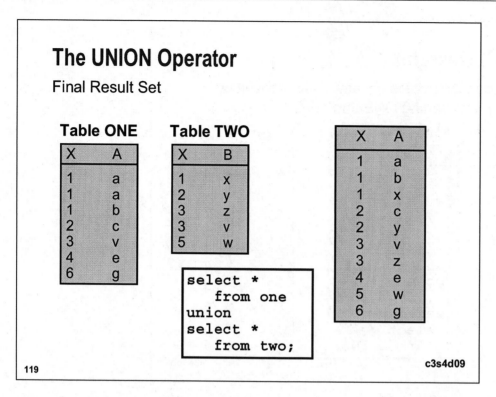

The UNION Operator

Final Result Set

Table ONE

X	A
1	a
1	a
1	b
2	c
3	v
4	e
6	g

Table TWO

X	B
1	x
2	y
3	z
3	v
5	w

X	A
1	a
1	b
1	x
2	c
2	y
3	v
3	z
4	e
5	w
6	g

```
select *
    from one
union
select *
    from two;
```

119   c3s4d09

Would the addition of the ALL keyword make any difference in this example?

Notice the overlay of columns A and B.

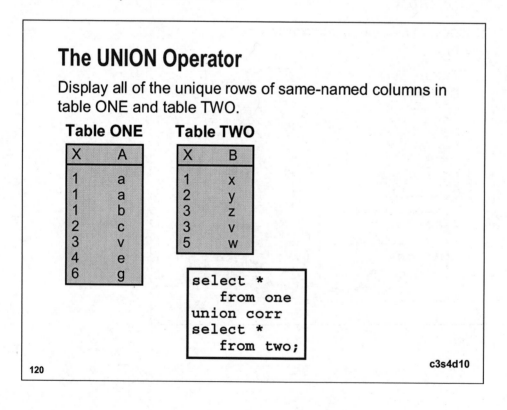

The UNION Operator

Display all of the unique rows of same-named columns in table ONE and table TWO.

Table ONE

X	A
1	a
1	a
1	b
2	c
3	v
4	e
6	g

Table TWO

X	B
1	x
2	y
3	z
3	v
5	w

```
select *
    from one
union corr
select *
    from two;
```

120   c3s4d10

The UNION Operator

The SQL processor creates an intermediate result by concatenating and sorting data from the first column.

Table ONE

X	A
1	a
1	a
1	b
2	c
3	v
4	e
6	g

Table TWO

X	B
1	x
2	y
3	z
3	v
5	w

X
1
1
1
1
2
2
3
3
3
3
4
5
6

```
select *
    from one
union corr
select *
    from two;
```

121

c3s4d10

The UNION Operator

The SQL processor removes duplicate rows from the intermediate result to generate the final result.

Table ONE

X	A
1	a
1	a
1	b
2	c
3	v
4	e
6	g

Table TWO

X	B
1	x
2	y
3	z
3	v
5	w

X
1
2
3
4
5
6

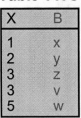

```
select *
    from one
union corr
select *
    from two;
```

122

c3s4d10

The UNION Operator

Example: Display the total miles traveled, total bonus points earned, and total bonus points used by frequent flyers.

Output

```
Points and Miles Traveled by Frequent Flyers

     Total Points Earned :     11,083,463
     Total Points Used   :      4,429,670
     Total Miles Traveled:     10,477,963
```

123

The UNION Operator

```
title 'Points and Miles Traveled '
      'by Frequent Flyers';
select 'Total Points Earned :',
       sum(PointsEarned) format=comma12.
   from airline.frequentflyers
          union all
select 'Total Points Used   :',
       sum(PointsUsed) format=comma12.
   from airline.frequentflyers
          union all
select 'Total Miles Traveled:',
       sum(MilesTraveled) format=comma12.
   from airline.frequentflyers;
```

124   c3s4d11

In this example, the keyword ALL is used to control the sorting by specifying that PROC SQL make one pass only.

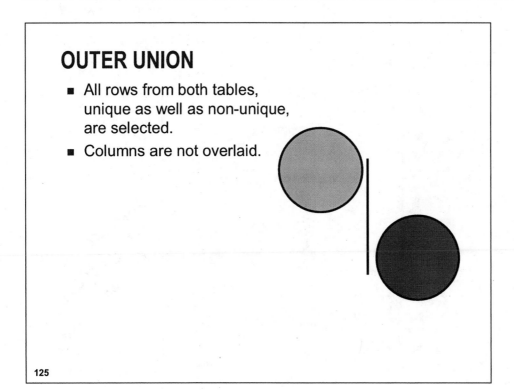

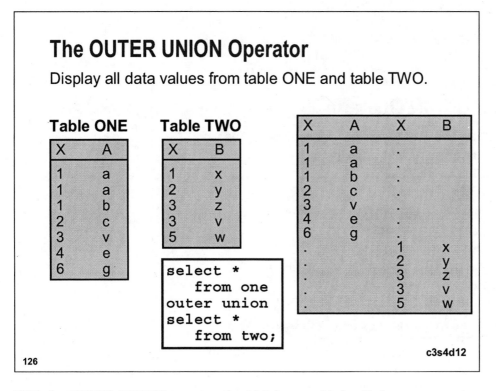

With the OUTER UNION operator, the ALL keyword is implied.

The OUTER UNION Operator

Display all data values from table ONE and table TWO, but overlay common columns.

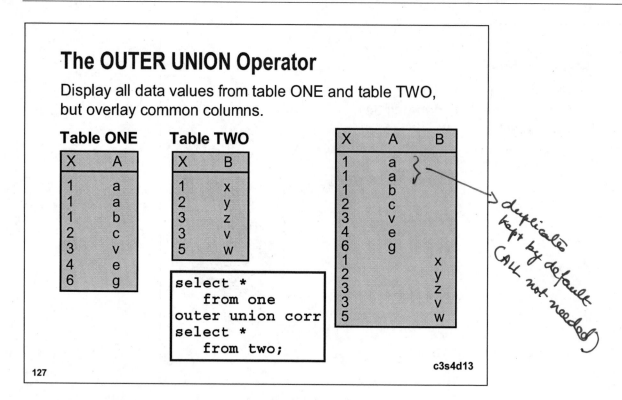

Table ONE

X	A
1	a
1	a
1	b
2	c
3	v
4	e
6	g

Table TWO

X	B
1	x
2	y
3	z
3	v
5	w

```
select *
    from one
outer union corr
select *
    from two;
```

X	A	B
1	a	
1	a	
1	b	
2	c	
3	v	
4	e	
6	g	
1		x
2		y
3		z
3		v
5		w

duplicates kept by default (ALL not needed)

127   c3s4d13

Common columns can be overlaid using the CORR keyword.

The same result is obtained by using a DATA step with a SET statement.

The OUTER UNION Operator

Example: Display the employee numbers, job codes, and salaries of all mechanics.

```
select *
    from airline.mechanicslevel1
        outer union corr
select *
    from airline.mechanicslevel2
        outer union corr
select *
    from airline.mechanicslevel3;
```

128   c3s4d14

The OUTER UNION Operator

Partial Output

Employee Number	Job Code	Salary
1400	ME1	$41,677
1403	ME1	$39,301
1120	ME1	$40,067
1121	ME1	$40,757
1412	ME1	$38,919
1200	ME1	$38,942
1995	ME1	$40,334
1418	ME1	$39,207
1653	ME2	$49,151
1782	ME2	$49,483

129

SQL versus Traditional SAS Programming

The following programs produce the same report:

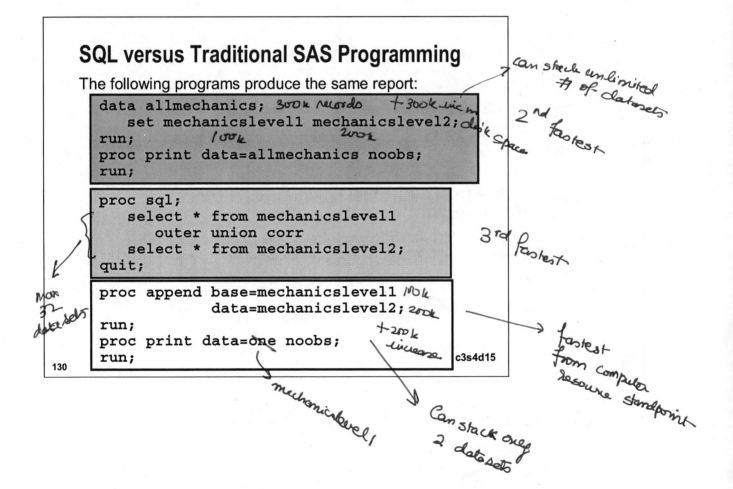

```
data allmechanics;
    set mechanicslevel1 mechanicslevel2;
run;
proc print data=allmechanics noobs;
run;
```

```
proc sql;
    select * from mechanicslevel1
        outer union corr
    select * from mechanicslevel2;
quit;
```

```
proc append base=mechanicslevel1
            data=mechanicslevel2;
run;
proc print data=one noobs;
run;
```

c3s4d15

130

Handwritten annotations:
- data allmechanics; 300k records + 300k records; disk space — Can stack unlimited # of datasets — 2nd fastest
- set mechanicslevel1 (100k) mechanicslevel2 (200k)
- proc sql ... — Max 32 datasets — 3rd fastest
- proc append base=mechanicslevel1 (100k) data=mechanicslevel2 (200k) +200k increase — fastest from computer resource standpoint — Can stack only 2 datasets
- proc print data=one → mechanicslevel1

Comparing Methods of Combining Tables Vertically

- PROC APPEND is the fastest method of performing a simple concatenation of two tables. The BASE= table is not completely read; only the DATA= table is completely read.
- When logical conditions are involved, you can choose either the DATA step or PROC SQL.
- SQL set operators generally require more computer resources, but the other operators are more convenient and flexible.

continued...

131

Comparing Methods of Combining Tables Vertically

- With the DATA step, you can process an unlimited number of tables at one time.
- With SQL set operators, you can work on only two tables at a time.
- If multiple DATA steps are required to perform the task, consider using PROC SQL.
- If you are unsure which method is best, use the techniques discussed in Chapter 5 to benchmark.

132

 Although set operators work on only two tables at a time, you can chain multiple operators together, as in the mechanics example demonstrated earlier in this section.

 **Exercises**

Submit a LIBNAME statement to assign the libref **airline** to the course SAS data library.

TSO: `libname airline '.sql.sasdata';`

Directory-based systems: `libname airline '.';`

7. **Using Set Operators**

Create a report that displays only the domestic (noninternational) flight numbers and destinations. **airline.marchflights** contains data on **all** flights. **airline.internationalflights** contains data on only the **international** flights.

FlightNumber	Destination
114	LAX
183	WAS
202	ORD
290	WAS
302	WAS
308	ORD
416	WAS
431	LAX
439	
439	LAX
523	ORD
829	WAS
872	LAX
921	DFW
982	DFW

8. Handling a Complex Query

airline.payrollchanges and **airline.staffchanges** contain data on employees with changes in job code or salary, as well as data on new employees. Create a report that displays information on new employees only, as shown below.

EmpID	FirstName	LastName	State	Job Code	DateOfHire
1447	AMY	BRIDESTON	NY	FA1	01NOV2000
1998	JIM	POWELL	NY	SCP	05NOV2000

To produce this report, break the problem into several steps.

a. Find the **EmpID** values of the new employees. Data on long-standing employees is stored in **airline.staffmaster**. **airline.staffchanges** contains data on existing employees with status changes, plus new employees.

b. In a separate query, display the **EmpID**, **FirstName**, **LastName**, and **State** columns from **airline.staffchanges**, with the **JobCode** and **DateOfHire** columns from **airline.payrollchanges**. (Six rows are displayed.)

c. Combine the two queries in parts **a** and **b**, so that the results of **b** (displaying six employees) are subset to display only employees returned from **a**.

3.5 Chapter Summary

PROC SQL provides many ways to combine data from multiple tables. Join operations enable you to combine tables horizontally using a key value. You can use an inner join to retrieve rows from up to 32 tables. Conceptually, PROC SQL forms a Cartesian product (all possible combinations of rows) and then selects the rows that satisfy the WHERE expression(s).

Outer joins enable you to select matching rows as well as nonmatching rows. A left join selects matching rows plus nonmatching rows from the left table. A right join selects matching rows plus nonmatching rows from the right table. A full join selects matching rows plus nonmatching rows from both tables (similar to a DATA step merge). The COALESCE function is available to overlay columns in the output. You can assign an alias to a table to simplify qualified column references in the query.

An in-line view is created when the FROM clause contains a query expression instead of actual table names, and exists only during the execution of the query.

You can use set operators to combine two tables vertically, that is, one table displayed immediately above the other. The EXCEPT operator selects unique rows from the first table that are not found in the second table. The INTERSECT operator selects unique rows found in both tables. The UNION operator selects all unique rows from both tables. The OUTER UNION operator concatenates the two tables. You can use the ALL keyword to prevent duplicate rows from being eliminated. The CORRESPONDING keyword forces PROC SQL to compare columns by name rather than by position.

General form of an inner join:

```
SELECT column-1, column-2, …
       FROM table-1, table-2, …
       WHERE join-condition(s)
           <AND other subsetting conditions>
       <other clauses>;
```

General form of an outer join:

```
SELECT column-1, column-2, …
       FROM table-1
           LEFT|RIGHT|FULL JOIN
               table-2
           ON join-condition(s)
       <other clauses>;
```

General form of an inner join that uses the ON clause:

```
SELECT *
       FROM table-1 INNER JOIN table-2
       ON table-1.x = table-2.x;
```

General form of a left join:

```
SELECT column-1, column-2, …
       FROM table-1 LEFT JOIN table-2
       ON expression;
```

General form of a right join:

```
SELECT column-1, column-2, ...
    FROM table-1 RIGHT JOIN table-2
    ON expression;
```

General form of a full join:

```
SELECT column-1, column-2, ...
    FROM table-1 FULL JOIN table-2
    ON expression;
```

General form of a set operation:

```
SELECT column-1, column-2, ...
    FROM table-1
set-operator
SELECT column-1, column-2, ...
    FROM table-2;
```

Set operators:

EXCEPT

INTERSECT

UNION

OUTER UNION

3.6 Solutions to Exercises

1. Combining Data from Two Tables

```
proc sql;
title 'Employees with > 20 Years of Service';
title2 'as of 01JAN2001';
select FirstName,
       LastName
   from airline.staffmaster as s,
        airline.payrollmaster as p
   where s.EmpID=p.EmpID
      and int(('01jan2001'd - DateOfHire)/365.25) > 20
   order by LastName;
quit;
title;
```

2. Combining Data from Two Tables

```
proc sql;
title 'Employees with > 20 Years of Service';
title2 'as of 01JAN2001';
select FirstName,
       LastName,
       int(('01jan2001'd - DateOfHire) / 365.25)
          as YearsOfService
   from airline.staffmaster as s,
        airline.payrollmaster as p
   where s.EmpID=p.EmpID
      and calculated YearsOfService > 20
   order by LastName;
quit;
title;
```

3. Combining Data from Two Tables

```
proc sql;
title 'Capacity Figures for International Flights';
select i.FlightNumber,
       i.Date,
       i.Boarded,
       PassengerCapacity,
       i.Boarded / PassengerCapacity as Percent
          format=percent5.
   from airline.internationalflights as i,
        airline.marchflights as m
   where i.FlightNumber=m.FlightNumber
      and i.Date=m.Date
   order by 1, 2;
quit;
title;
```

4. Summarizing Data from Two Tables

```
proc sql;
title 'Salary Statistics by State and Job Code';
select State,
       JobCode,
       count(*) as TotalEmployees,
       avg(Salary) as AverageSalary
          format=dollar11.2,
       max(Salary) as MaximumSalary
          format=dollar11.2,
       min(Salary) as MinimumSalary
          format=dollar11.2
   from airline.staffmaster as s,
        airline.payrollmaster as p
   where s.EmpID=p.EmpID
   group by State, JobCode
   order by State, JobCode;
quit;
```

5. Combining Data from Multiple Tables (Optional)

```
proc sql;
title 'Flight Schedule for Airline Employees';
select f.FlightNumber,
       f.Date,
       FirstName format=$10.,
       LastName format=$10.,
       f.EmpID,
       DepartureTime as DepTime,
       f.Destination as Dest
   from airline.staffmaster as s,
        airline.flightschedule as f,
        airline.marchflights as m
   where s.EmpID=f.EmpID
     and f.FlightNumber=m.FlightNumber
     and f.Date=m.Date
   order by 1, 2, 4, 3;
quit;
title;
```

6. Combining Data from Multiple Tables (Optional)

```
proc sql;
title 'Flight Attendants Schedule for Copenhagen';
select distinct FirstName, LastName
   from airline.staffmaster as s,
        airline.payrollmaster as p,
        airline.flightschedule as f
   where s.EmpID=p.EmpID
      and s.EmpID=f.EmpID
      and JobCode like 'FA_'
      and Destination='CPH'
   order by LastName;
quit;
title;
```

7. Using Set Operators

```
proc sql;
select FlightNumber, Destination
   from airline.marchflights
except
select FlightNumber, Destination
   from airline.internationalflights;
quit;
```

8. Handling a Complex Query

    a.

```
proc sql;
select EmpID
   from airline.staffchanges
except all
select EmpID
   from airline.staffmaster;
quit;
```

    b.

```
proc sql;
select s.EmpID,
       FirstName,
       LastName,
       State,
       JobCode,
       DateOfHire
   from airline.staffchanges as s,
        airline.payrollchanges as p
   where s.EmpID = p.EmpID;
quit;
```

c.

```
proc sql;
select s.EmpID,
       FirstName,
       LastName,
       State,
       JobCode,
       DateOfHire
   from airline.staffchanges as s,
        airline.payrollchanges as p
   where s.EmpID = p.EmpID
      and s.EmpID in
          (select EmpID
             from airline.staffchanges
           except all
           select EmpID
             from airline.staffmaster);
quit;
```

Chapter 4   Creating and Modifying Tables and Views

4.1 Creating Tables

Objectives

- Define the column structure of a new table or use the column definitions from an existing table.
- Load data into a new table.
- Create a new table from the results of a query.

3

Creating Tables

Use the CREATE TABLE statement in three ways.

Creates an empty table (Methods 1A and 1B).

CREATE TABLE *table-name (column-name type(length), <column-name type(length)>,...);*

CREATE TABLE *table-name* **LIKE** *table-name;*

CREATE TABLE *table-name* **AS** *query-expression;*

Populates table with a query result (Method 2).

4

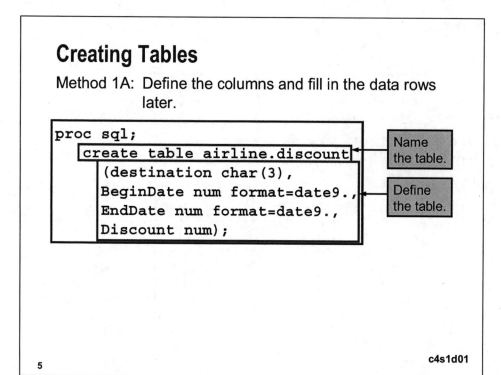

Creating Tables

Method 1A: Define the columns and fill in the data rows
             later.

```
proc sql;
   create table airline.discount
      (destination char(3),
      BeginDate num format=date9.,
      EndDate num format=date9.,
      Discount num);
```

Name
the table.

Define
the table.

5   c4s1d01

Defining Columns

PROC SQL accepts

- types of CHARACTER or VARCHAR, but interprets
  both as SAS CHARACTER. Default length is 8 bytes.

- types of INTEGER, SMALLINT, DECIMAL, NUMERIC,
  FLOAT, REAL, and DOUBLE PRECISION,
  interpreting all as SAS NUMERIC with a length of 8
  bytes.

- a type of DATE, interpreted as a SAS NUMERIC, with
  a length of 8 bytes and a DATE. informat and format.

6

Although SAS reads all of the above-mentioned data types, only CHARACTER and NUMERIC are used
in SAS tables.

Defining Columns: More Examples

Method 1A:

```
proc sql;
   create table x
       (Name char(20),
        BirthDate date,
        Salary num format=comma10.2);
```

#	Variable	Type	Len	Format
1	Name	Char	20	
2	BirthDate	Num	8	DATE.
3	Salary	Num	8	COMMA10.2

c4s1d02

7

The table created above does not contain any rows. Use this method when the table you want to create is unlike any other existing table.

Defining Columns: More Examples

Method 1A:

```
proc sql;
   create table y
       (Dept varchar,
        Code integer label='Dept Code');
```

#	Variable	Type	Len	Label
1	Dept	Char	8	
2	Code	Num	8	Dept Code

c4s1d03

8

Defining Columns

Example: Create a table to store discounts for certain
          destinations and time periods in March. Define
          columns for destination, discount, and
          beginning and ending dates of the discount.

```
proc sql;
   create table discount
       (Destination char(3),
        BeginDate date label='BEGINS',
        EndDate date label='ENDS',
        Discount num);
```

Partial Log

```
NOTE:Table WORK.DISCOUNT created, with 0 rows
and 4 columns.
```

9   c4s1d04

Creating Tables

Method 1B: Copy a table. Use column definitions from
            another table and fill in the rows of data later.

```
proc sql;
   create table airline.delaycat
       (drop=DelayCategory DestinationType)
       like airline.flightdelays;
```

The columns
in this table
are copied
to the new table.

10   c4s1d05
                                                        ...

Use Method 1A to create tables containing columns that do not already exist in other tables.
In other words, you define your own columns.

Creating Tables

Method 2: Store a query result in a table that defines both columns and rows.

```
proc sql;
    create table airline.fa as
       select LastName, FirstName, Salary
          from airline.payrollmaster,
               airline.staffmaster
          where payrollmaster.EmpID
                =staffmaster.EmpID
                and JobCode contains 'FA' ;
       select *
          from airline.fa;
```

c4s1d06

11

This method is particularly helpful when you create subsets or supersets of tables.

Use of the CREATE TABLE statement shuts off the automatic report generation. Also, this is the only method of the three that **both** creates **and** populates a table at the same time.

✐   Use this method when the table you want to create is similar or identical to another existing table.

Loading Data into a Table

Partial Output

The SAS System		
LastName	FirstName	Salary
ARTHUR	BARBARA	$46,040
CAHILL	MARSHALL	$40,001
CARTER	DOROTHY	$46,346
COOPER	ANTHONY	$45,104
DEAN	SHARON	$46,787
DUNLAP	DONNA	$40,443
EATON	ALICIA	$38,902
FIELDS	DIANA	$32,448
FLETCHER	MARIE	$31,436
GOMEZ	ALAN	$31,175

12

Loading Data into a Table

Method A: The SET Clause

```
INSERT INTO table-name
    SET column-name=value,column-name=value,...;
```

Method B: The VALUES Clause

```
INSERT INTO table-name <(column list)>
    VALUES (value,value,value, ...);
```

Method C: A Query-expression

```
INSERT INTO table-name <(column list)>
    SELECT columns FROM table-name
```

13

Loading Data into a Table

After the table is created, you can enter rows of data and use the INSERT statement with one of three methods.

Method A: The SET Clause

Populate Discount with these values.

```
proc sql;
   insert into discount
        set Destination='LHR',
            BeginDate='01MAR2000'd,
            EndDate='05MAR2000'd,Discount=.33
        set Destination='CPH',
            BeginDate='03MAR2000'd,
            EndDate='10MAR2000'd, Discount=.15;
```

14   c4s1d07

You can nest a SELECT statement within a SET statement, as follows:

```
proc sql;
   insert into discount
        set Destination='LHR', BeginDate=(select max(Date)
            from airline.flightdelays);
```

Loading Data into a Table

Method B: The VALUES Clause

```
proc sql;
   insert into discount
      values('LHR','01MAR2000'd,
             '05MAR2000'd,.33)
      values('CPH','03MAR2000'd,
             '10MAR2000'd,.15);
```

15

c4s1d08

Loading Data into a Table

Method C: A Query-expression

```
proc sql;
   insert into discount(Destination,Discount)
      select Destination, Rate*.25
         from airline.fares
         where Type='special';
```

16

c4s1d09

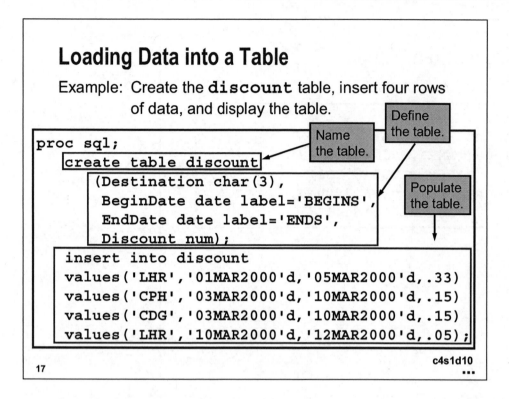

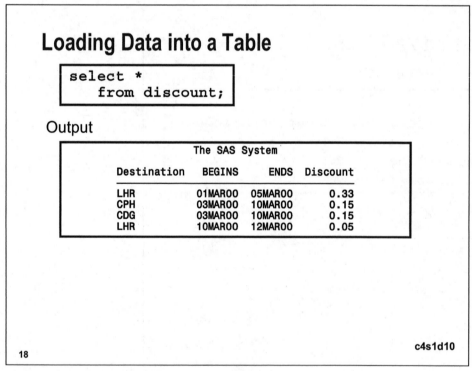

You can use PROC PRINT in place of the final SELECT statement.

Integrity Constraints

- Integrity constraints are rules that table modifications must follow to guarantee validity of data.
- You can preserve the consistency and correctness of data by specifying integrity constraints for a SAS data file.
- SAS uses the integrity constraints to validate data when you insert or update the values of a variable for which you have defined integrity constraints.

19

Integrity Constraints

Integrity constraints

- are part of Version 8 of Base SAS software
- follow ANSI standards
- cannot be defined for views
- can be specified when a table is created or later when a table contains data.

20

Integrity constraints can be defined for historical versions of generation data sets using the DATASETS procedure but cannot be added using the SQL procedure.

Five Integrity Constraints

General:

- NOT NULL
- CHECK
- UNIQUE

Referential:

- PRIMARY KEY
- FOREIGN KEY

21

NOT NULL	means that data is required and ensures that corresponding columns have non-missing values in each row.
CHECK	specifies what values may be entered in a column. If a user attempts to enter data that violates this constraint, SAS rejects the value.
UNIQUE	ensures that every value in a column is unique. The same column can be defined as NULL, but only a single null value is allowed per UNIQUE column.
PRIMARY KEY	identifies the column as the table's primary key. Only unique values are permitted and the primary key cannot contain missing values.
FOREIGN KEY	links one or more columns in a table to a specific column in another table by matching a foreign key in one table with the primary key in another table. This parent/child relationship limits modifications made to both primary and foreign keys. The only acceptable values for a foreign key are values of the primary key or missing values.

Using PROC SQL to Create Integrity Constraints

General form of PROC SQL using integrity constraints:

PROC SQL;
  CREATE TABLE *table*
    (*column-specification*,…
     <*constraint-specification*,…>);

22

Using PROC SQL to Create Integrity Constraints

Example: Re-create the **discount** table with an
      integrity constraint to limit ticket discounting.

```
proc sql;
   create table discount
      (Destination char(3),
       BeginDate date label='BEGINS',
       EndDate date label='ENDS',
       Discount num,
       CONSTRAINT ok_discount check
          (Discount le .5));
```

c4s1d11

23

Using PROC SQL to Create Integrity Constraints

Example: Insert two rows using the default
UNDO_POLICY option (required).

```
proc sql;
   insert into discount
     values('CDG','03MAR2000'd,'10MAR2000'd,.15)
     values('LHR','10MAR2000'd,'12MAR2000'd,.55);
```

Stockholders might not tolerate excessive airline generosity!

24   c4s1d12

Using PROC SQL to Create Integrity Constraints

Partial Log

```
proc sql;
   insert into discount
       values('CDG','03MAR2000'd,'10MAR2000'd,.15)
       values('LHR','10MAR2000'd,'12MAR2000'd,.55);
ERROR: Add/Update failed for data set WORK.DISCOUNT because data
value(s) do not comply with integrity constraint ok_discount.
NOTE: This insert failed while attempting to add data from VALUES
clause 2 to the data set.
NOTE: Deleting the successful inserts before error noted above to
restore table to a consistent state.
```

0 rows inserted.

25

Rollbacks

If an INSERT or UPDATE statement experiences an error while it processes the statement, then the inserts or updates that were completed up to the point of the error by that statement can be undone by use of the UNDO_POLICY option.

26

Rollbacks with the UNDO_POLICY Option

- UNDO_POLICY=REQUIRED (the default)

  undoes all inserts or updates that have been done to the point of the error. Sometimes the UNDO operation cannot be done reliably.

- UNDO_POLICY=NONE

  prevents any updates or inserts from violating a constraint.

- UNDO_POLICY=OPTIONAL

  reverses any updates or inserts that it can reverse reliably.

27

The ROLLBACK statement, although an ANSI standard, is not currently supported in the SQL procedure.

UNDO_POLICY=REQUIRED

PROC SQL performs UNDO processing for INSERT and UPDATE statements.

If the UNDO operation cannot be done reliably, PROC SQL does not execute the statement and issues an ERROR message.

UNDO cannot be attempted reliably in the following situations:

1. A SAS data set opened with CNTLLEV=RECORD can enable other users to update newly inserted records. An error during the insert deletes the record that the other user inserted.

2. A SAS/ACCESS view is not able to rollback the changes made by this statement without rolling back other changes at the same time.

Default: UNDO_POLICY=REQUIRED

UNDO_POLICY=NONE

PROC SQL skips records that cannot be inserted or updated, and writes to the SAS log a warning message similar to that written by PROC APPEND.

UNDO_POLICY=OPTIONAL

PROC SQL performs UNDO processing if it can be done reliably. If the UNDO cannot be done reliably, then no UNDO processing is attempted.

This option is a combination of the first two. If UNDO can be done reliably, then it is done. PROC SQL proceeds as if UNDO_POLICY=REQUIRED is in effect. Otherwise, it proceeds as if UNDO_POLICY=NONE was specified.

Using PROC SQL to Create Integrity Constraints

Example: Insert two rows using UNDO_POLICY=NONE.

```
proc sql undo_policy=none ;
 insert into discount
   values('CDG','03MAR2000'd,'10MAR2000'd,.15)
   values('LHR','10MAR2000'd,'12MAR2000'd,.55);
```

28   c4s1d13

✎   An alternative is to create constraints using the DATASETS procedure.

Using PROC SQL to Create Integrity Constraints

Partial Log

```
WARNING: The SQL option UNDO_POLICY=REQUIRED is not in effect.
If an error is detected when processing this INSERT statement,
that error will not cause the entire statement to fail.
ERROR: Add/Update failed for data set WORK.DISCOUNT because data
value(s) do not comply with integrity constraint ok_discount.
NOTE: This insert failed while attempting to add data from VALUES
clause 2 to the data set.
NOTE: 2 rows were inserted into WORK.DISCOUNT. Of these 1 row was
rejected as an ERROR, leaving 1 row that was inserted successfully
```

1 of 2 rows inserted successfully.

29

Documenting Table and View Definitions and Integrity Constraints

The DESCRIBE statement displays the definition of the view or CREATE TABLE statement of a table.

General form of the DESCRIBE statement:

```
PROC SQL;
     DESCRIBE TABLE table-name<,table-name>...;
     DESCRIBE VIEW proc-sql-view <,proc-sql-view>...;
     DESCRIBE TABLE CONSTRAINTS table-name
                    <,table-name> ...;
```

30

The DESCRIBE TABLE statement (without the CONSTRAINTS keyword) writes a CREATE TABLE statement to the SAS log for the specified table regardless of how the table was originally created (for example, with a DATA step).

If the table contains an index, CREATE INDEX statements for those indexes are also written to the SAS log. (A discussion of indexes is in Section 4.3.)

Documenting Table Definitions and Integrity Constraints

Example: Show the constraints for the **discount** table.

```
proc sql;
    describe table discount;
```

31   c4s1d14

Documenting Table Definitions and Integrity Constraints

```
NOTE: SQL table WORK.DISCOUNT was created like:

create table WORK.DISCOUNT( bufsize=4096 )
  (
  Destination char(3),
  BeginDate num format=DATE. informat=DATE. label='BEGINS',
  EndDate num format=DATE. informat=DATE. label='ENDS',
  Discount num
  );
      -----Alphabetic List of Integrity Constraints-----


            Integrity              Where
      #     Constraint    Type     Clause
      _____

      1     ok_discount   Check    discount<=0.5
```

32

4.2 Creating Views

Objectives

- Create an SQL view and understand how it is best used.

34

Creating a View

A PROC SQL view

- is a stored query. It contains no rows of data.
- can be used in SAS programs in place of an actual SAS data file.
- can be derived from one or more tables, PROC SQL views, DATA step views, or SAS/ACCESS views.
- extracts underlying data when used, thus accessing the most current data.

35

Views are not separate copies of the data and are referred to as *virtual tables* because they do not exist as independent entities as do real tables. It may be helpful to think of a view as a movable frame or window through which you can see the data.

Thus, when the view is referenced by a SAS procedure or in a DATA step, it is executed, and conceptually, an internal table is built. PROC SQL processes this internal table as if it were any other table.

Creating a View

General form of the CREATE VIEW statement:

CREATE VIEW *view-name* **AS**
   query-expression;

Creating a View

Example: Create a view containing personal information for flight attendants. Have the view always return the employee's age as of the current date.

```
proc sql;
   create view airline.faview as
      select LastName,FirstName, Gender,
              int((today()-DateOfBirth)/365.25)
                as Age,
              substr(JobCode,3,1) as Level,
              Salary
         from airline.payrollmaster,
              airline.staffmaster
         where JobCode contains 'FA' and
              staffmaster.EmpID=
              payrollmaster.EmpID;
```

c4s2d01

37

In this example, the view **airline.faview** creates a virtual table from the accompanying SELECT statement. Although the underlying tables, **airline.payrollmaster** and **airline.staffmaster**, can change, the instructions, which comprise the view, stay constant. Further, when this PROC SQL step is executed, SAS does not actually execute the SELECT statement following the AS keyword, but instead partially compiles and stores the SELECT statement in a data file with a member type of VIEW.

If the above example is modified to a CREATE TABLE statement and the alias **Age** is omitted, SAS creates a sequentially suffixed variable, starting with _TEMA001. The librefs for the tables in the FROM clause are optional in this case. It is assumed that the contributing tables are stored in the same library as the view itself, unless otherwise specified.

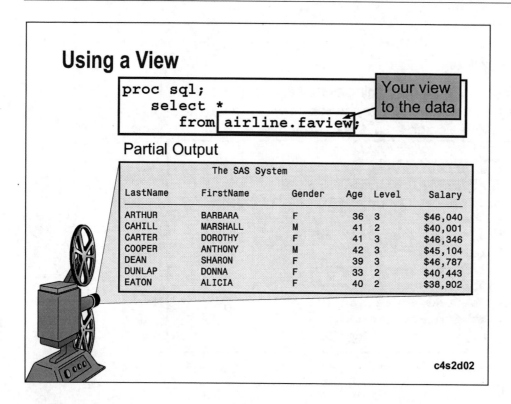

Using a View

```
proc sql;
   select *
      from airline.faview;
```

Your view to the data

Partial Output

```
                     The SAS System

LastName        FirstName       Gender   Age   Level      Salary

ARTHUR          BARBARA         F         36   3        $46,040
CAHILL          MARSHALL        M         41   2        $40,001
CARTER          DOROTHY         F         41   3        $46,346
COOPER          ANTHONY         M         42   3        $45,104
DEAN            SHARON          F         39   3        $46,787
DUNLAP          DONNA           F         33   2        $40,443
EATON           ALICIA          F         40   2        $38,902
```

c4s2d02

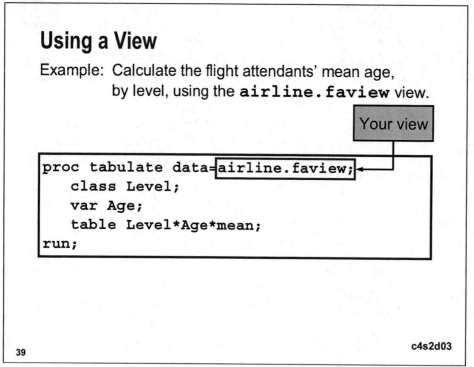

Using a View

Example: Calculate the flight attendants' mean age,
          by level, using the **airline.faview** view.

Your view

```
proc tabulate data=airline.faview;
   class Level;
   var Age;
   table Level*Age*mean;
run;
```

39   c4s2d03

In both of the above examples, it only appears that the PROC SQL view, **airline.faview**, is a table because the view name itself is used in the same way as a SAS table name. However, it is **not** a table, but a stored query-expression only. Both tables and views are considered SAS data sets.

Using a View

PROC TABULATE Output

Level		
1	2	3
Age	Age	Age
Mean	Mean	Mean
39.82	43.81	45.43

40

Administering Views

Example: Write the view definition for **airline.fa** to the SAS log.

```
proc sql;
   describe view airline.faview;
```

```
NOTE: SQL view AIRLINE.FAVIEW is defined as:

select LastName, FirstName, Gender,
       INT((TODAY()-DateOfBirth)/365.25) as Age,
       SUBSTR(JobCode, 3, 1) as Level, Salary
   from AIRLINE.PAYROLLMASTER, AIRLINE.STAFFMASTER
     where JobCode contains 'FA' and
       (staffmaster.EmpID=payrollmaster.EmpID);
```

c4s2d04

41

Why Use Views?

You can

- access the most current data in changing tables, DATA step views, or SAS/ACCESS views
- pull together data from multiple database tables or even different databases
- simplify complex query-expressions and prevent users from altering code
- avoid storing a SAS copy of a large table.

42

Administering Views: Some General Guidelines

- Avoid the ORDER BY clause in a view definition. Otherwise, the data must be sorted each time the view is referenced.
- If the same data is used many times in one program, create a table rather than a view.
- Avoid specifying two-level names in the FROM clause when you create a permanent view that resides in the same library as the contributing table(s).

43

Administering Views

Example:

```
proc sql;
   create view sasdata.master as
      select *
         from sasdata.payrollmaster;
```

It is better to omit the libref.

c4s2d05

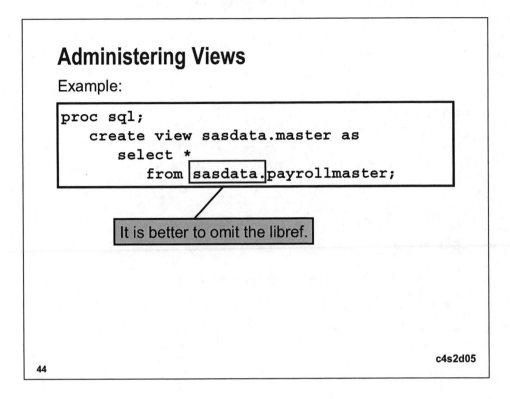

Administering Views: Omitting the Libref

Example:

```
proc sql;
   create view sasdata.master as
      select *
         from payrollmaster;
```

This looks like work.payrollmaster,...

... but is **in reality** sasdata.payrollmaster.

c4s2d06

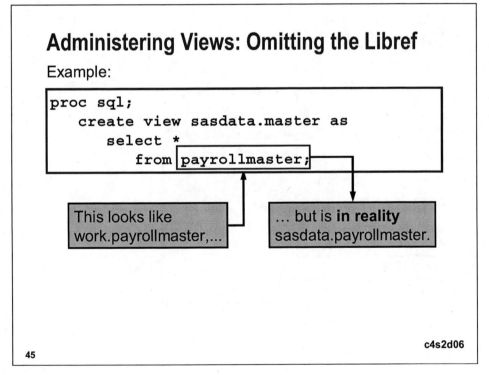

Administering Views: Why Is It Better to Omit the Libref?

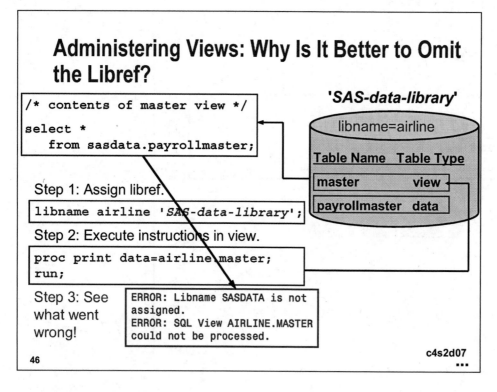

```
/* contents of master view */
select *
   from sasdata.payrollmaster;
```

'SAS-data-library'

libname=airline

Table Name	Table Type
master	view
payrollmaster	data

Step 1: Assign libref.

```
libname airline 'SAS-data-library';
```

Step 2: Execute instructions in view.

```
proc print data=airline.master;
run;
```

Step 3: See what went wrong!

```
ERROR: Libname SASDATA is not
assigned.
ERROR: SQL View AIRLINE.MASTER
could not be processed.
```

46   c4s2d07
                                                         •••

Administering Views: Why Is It Better to Omit the Libref?

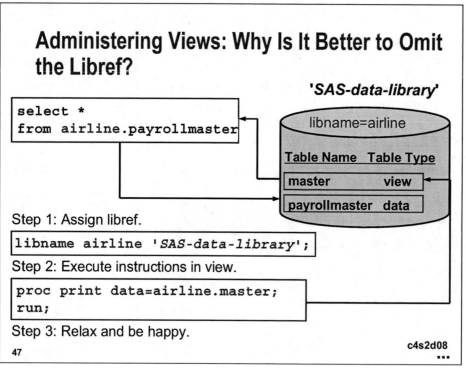

```
select *
from airline.payrollmaster
```

'SAS-data-library'

libname=airline

Table Name	Table Type
master	view
payrollmaster	data

Step 1: Assign libref.

```
libname airline 'SAS-data-library';
```

Step 2: Execute instructions in view.

```
proc print data=airline.master;
run;
```

Step 3: Relax and be happy.

47   c4s2d08
                                                         •••

Creating Views

An alternative: Embed the LIBNAME statement within a USING clause.

```
CREATE VIEW proc-sql-view AS query-expression
        <USING statement<, libname-clause> ... > ;
```

This enables you to store a SAS libref in the view and does not conflict with an identically named libref in the SAS session.

48

Administering Views: Using the Embedded LIBNAME Statement

```
libname sasdata 'SAS-data-library-one';
libname airline 'SAS-data-library-two';

proc sql;
   create view sasdata.journeymen as
   select *
       from airline.payrollmaster
       where JobCode like '  2'
       using libname airline 'SAS-data-library-three';
quit;
proc print data = sasdata.journeymen ;
run;
```

3) ... overriding any earlier assignment for the duration of the view's execution.

2) ... the libref `airline` becomes active ...

1) While the view `sasdata.journeymen` is executing ...

4) After view executes, original libref assignment (3) is re-established and embedded assignment (2) is cleared.

c4s2d09

49

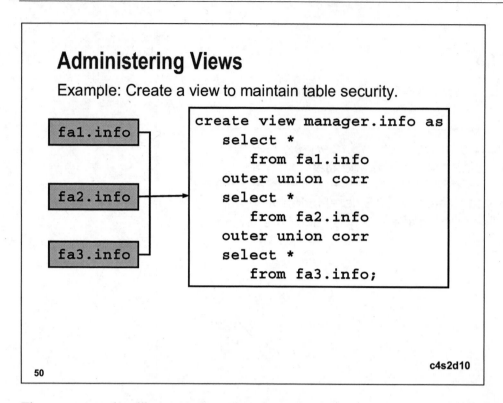

Administering Views

Example: Create a view to maintain table security.

```
create view manager.info as
    select *
        from fa1.info
    outer union corr
    select *
        from fa2.info
    outer union corr
    select *
        from fa3.info;
```

c4s2d10

50

The **manager** data library can be assigned access privileges at the operating system level. The access privilege prevents non-managerial flight attendants from reading the library, but permits managers (who are authorized to access all SAS data libraries) to view all information.

4.3   Creating Indexes

Objectives

- Create an index on a table.
- Understand how an index is best used.

52

Creating Indexes

An *index* is an auxiliary data structure that specifies the location of rows based on the values of one or more **key** columns.

The SQL procedure can utilize an available index to optimize subsetting or joining tasks.

53

The index is a structure that boosts program performance by serving as a logical pointer to a physical location of a given value.

Creating Indexes

	Indexed SAS Data Set			
Row	EmpID	Gender	JobCode	
1	1001	F	FA1	
2	1012	F	FA3	
3	1015	M	FA2	
.				
.				
11	1104	M	FA3	
.				
.				

Index File

Key Column=JobCode

Key Value	Location Page(row,row...)
FA1	1(1,4, ...) 2(...) ...
FA2	1(3,6, ...) 2(...) ...
FA3	1(2,11,...) 2(...) ...

Data Processed

ROW	EmpID	Gender	JobCode
2	1012	F	FA3
11	1104	M	FA3
.			

```
DATA or PROC Step

where JobCode='FA3';
```

54

Creating Indexes: Overview

Indexes provide fast access to small subsets of data...

```
proc sql;
   select *
      from airline.payrollmaster
      where JobCode='NA1';
```

One of many values
of the variable **JobCode**

55   c4s3d01

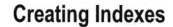 A small subset is ≤ 15%.

Creating Indexes: Overview

... and also enhance join performance.

```
proc sql;
    select *
        from airline.payrollmaster,
             airline.staffmaster
        where staffmaster.EmpID=
              payrollmaster.EmpID;
```

56

c4s3d02

When you subset data, you can select an index to optimize not only a WHERE clause with an equals comparison, but also a WHERE clause with the TRIM or SUBSTR function or the CONTAINS or LIKE operator.

Index Terminology

Two types of indexes are

- simple

    based on values of only one column

- composite

    based on values of more than one column
    concatenated to form a single value, for example,
    Date and **FlightNumber**.

Can have more than one
simple/composite index

57

 Index naming rules are the same as the rules for other SAS data files. Start with a letter or underscore, and continue with a combination of letters, characters, or numbers, with a 32-character maximum.

Index Terminology

A table can have the following:

- multiple simple and composite indexes
- character and numeric key columns

58

Creating an Index

- Designate the key column(s).
- Select a name for the index. A simple index must have the same name as the column.
- Specify if the index is to be unique.

```
proc sql;
   create unique index EmpID
   on airline.payrollmaster (EmpID);
```

59

c4s3d03
...

Creating an Index

General form of the CREATE INDEX statement:

> **CREATE <UNIQUE> INDEX** *index-name*
>   **ON** *table-name(column-name, column-name)*;

Precede the INDEX keyword with the UNIQUE keyword to define a unique index.

60

Use of the optional UNIQUE keyword ensures that values in the row are unique. If a table contains multiple occurrences of the same value, the UNIQUE keyword is not accepted and the index is not defined on that column. Similarly, if you already have a uniquely defined index on a column and attempt to add a duplicate value to the table, the row is not inserted. For example, an index can be created on a column containing driver license or social security numbers, and thereby can prevent duplicate additions.

Additional notes:

1. Indexes can be based on either a character or numeric variable.

2. You do not want to create two indexes on the same variable.

3. You can achieve improved index performance if you create the index on a pre-sorted data set.

4. A composite index cannot have the same name as a variable.

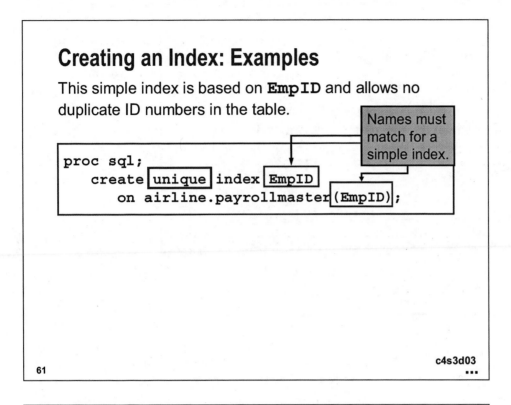

Creating an Index: Examples

This simple index is based on **EmpID** and allows no duplicate ID numbers in the table.

Names must match for a simple index.

```
proc sql;
   create unique index EmpID
        on airline.payrollmaster (EmpID);
```

61   c4s3d03
                                                                ...

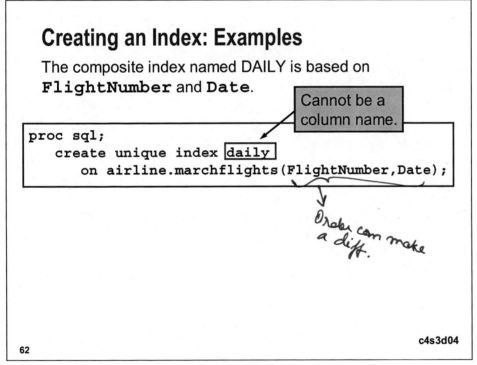

Creating an Index: Examples

The composite index named DAILY is based on **FlightNumber** and **Date**.

Cannot be a column name.

```
proc sql;
   create unique index daily
        on airline.marchflights(FlightNumber,Date);
```

Order can make a diff.

62   c4s3d04

To determine if an index is used, specify the SAS system option MSGLEVEL=I. A note appears in the SAS log when an index is selected for processing.

Indexing and Performance

Example: An index was created for the **JobCode**
column of **airline.payrollmaster**.
Use the MSGLEVEL=I system option to
determine which queries used the index.

```
options msglevel = i;
proc sql;
   select *
      from airline.payrollmaster
      where JobCode = 'NA1';
INFO:Index JobCode selected for WHERE clause optimization.

   select *
      from airline.payrollmaster
      where Salary gt 100000;
```

Applies to this WHERE clause only.

c4s3d05

63

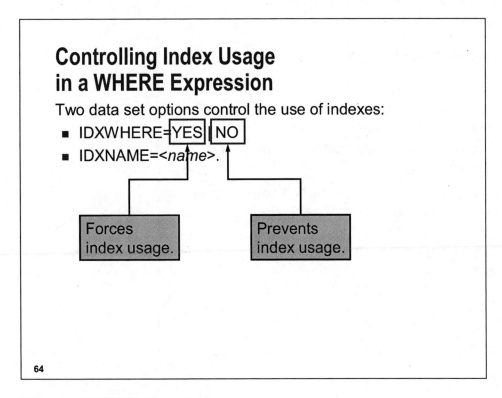

**Controlling Index Usage
in a WHERE Expression**

Two data set options control the use of indexes:

- IDXWHERE=YES│NO
- IDXNAME=<*name*>.

Forces
index usage.

Prevents
index usage.

64

When the IDXWHERE= option is

YES   SAS uses the best available index to process the WHERE expression, even if SAS estimates that sequential processing is faster.

NO   SAS processes the data sequentially even if SAS estimates that processing with an index is better.

When the IDXNAME= option is

<*name*>   SAS uses the named index regardless of performance estimates.

If you do not use the IDXWHERE= option, SAS chooses whether to use an index. You can use either the IDXWHERE= or the IDXNAME= data set option, but not both.

Indexing and Performance

Suggested guidelines for using indexes:

- Keep the number of indexes to a minimum to reduce disk storage and update costs.
- Do not create an index for small tables; sequential access is faster on small tables.
- Do not create an index based on columns with a small number of distinct values, for example, Male and Female.
- An index performs best when it retrieves a relatively small number of rows, that is, <15%.

65

Indexing and Performance: Tradeoffs

Benefits	Costs
■ Fast access to a small subset of data (<15%).	■ Extra CPU cycles and I/O operations to create an index.
■ Equijoins can be performed without internal sorts.	■ Extra disk space to store the index file.
■ Can enforce uniqueness.	■ Extra memory to load index pages and code for use.
■ BY group processing without sorting.	■ Extra CPU cycles and I/O operations to maintain the index.

66

 **Exercises**

Submit a LIBNAME statement to assign the libref **airline** to the course SAS data library.
(TSO only: DISP=SHR)

TSO: `libname airline '.sql.sasdata';`

Directory-based systems: `libname airline '.';`

1. **Creating a Table**

    A frequent flyer earns points for each mile traveled with the airline. After accumulating a certain number of points, the frequent flyer is eligible for an award. You can claim a better award with more accumulated points.

    a. Create a temporary table named **awards** to store award data. The table's columns must have the following attributes:

Name	Type	Length	Format	Label
ptsreqd	NUM	8		Points Required
rank	NUM	8	3.	
award	CHAR	25		

    b. Load the following data into the table:

ptsreqd	rank	award
2000	1	free night in hotel
10000	2	50% discount on flight
20000	3	free domestic flight
40000	4	free international flight

    c. Display the new table.

d. The `airline.frequentflyers` table contains the number of points each frequent flyer earned (`PointsEarned`) and used (`PointsUsed`). Determine all appropriate awards for each frequent flyer based on the number of remaining points for each frequent flyer. An individual can receive multiple awards. Award levels are found in the new `awards` table. Process only the frequent flyers who live in Arizona (`STATE`='AZ'). Order the report by `FFID`.

Output

```
                    Awards Available to AZ Frequent Flyers

                                     Available
          FFID    Name               Points  Award
         _____

          WD0227  FOSTER, GERALD        29079  50% discount on flight
          WD0227  FOSTER, GERALD        29079  free domestic flight
          WD0227  FOSTER, GERALD        29079  free night in hotel
          WD0646  BOSTIC, MARIE         64544  50% discount on flight
          WD0646  BOSTIC, MARIE         64544  free domestic flight
          WD0646  BOSTIC, MARIE         64544  free international flight
          WD0646  BOSTIC, MARIE         64544  free night in hotel
          WD3022  CAHILL, LEONARD       46386  50% discount on flight
          WD3022  CAHILL, LEONARD       46386  free night in hotel
          WD3022  CAHILL, LEONARD       46386  free international flight
          WD3022  CAHILL, LEONARD       46386  free domestic flight
          WD4382  O'NEAL, ALICE         35047  50% discount on flight
          WD4382  O'NEAL, ALICE         35047  free domestic flight
          WD4382  O'NEAL, ALICE         35047  free night in hotel
          WD6061  RODRIGUEZ, MARIA      20642  free night in hotel
          WD6061  RODRIGUEZ, MARIA      20642  50% discount on flight
          WD6061  RODRIGUEZ, MARIA      20642  free domestic flight
          WD6080  SMART, JONATHAN       16266  free night in hotel
          WD6080  SMART, JONATHAN       16266  50% discount on flight
          WD7208  LONG, CASEY           19443  free night in hotel
          WD7208  LONG, CASEY           19443  50% discount on flight
          WD8375  COOPER, ANTHONY        5507  free night in hotel
          WD9829  COOK, JENNIFER         4401  free night in hotel
```

e. (Optional) Determine which frequent flyers are not eligible for any award. Order the report by **FFID**. Include all states.

Output

```
┌─────────────────────────────────────────────────────────────┐
│            Frequent Flyers Ineligible for Awards            │
│                                                             │
│                                           Available         │
│            FFID        Name                Points           │
│                                                             │
│            WD0023   JACKSON, LAURA              -5          │
│            WD0231   GORDON, ANNE            -13054          │
│            WD0632   BROWN, JASON           -19367          │
│            WD1218   GRAHAM, MARY              -441          │
│            WD1637   NELSON, FELICIA         -6047          │
│            WD1700   WOOD, ALAN             -12836          │
│            WD1883   PENNINGTON, MICHAEL     -3957          │
│            WD2118   JOHNSON, ANTHONY          609          │
│            WD2741   EDGERTON, WAYNE        -29012          │
│            WD3129   FLOWERS, ANNETTE       -17635          │
│            WD3521   FIELDS, DIANA           -6151          │
│            WD4065   DONALDSON, KAREN        -6733          │
│            WD4781   HUNTER, CLYDE            1931          │
│            WD5020   BOYCE, RANDALL           1922          │
└─────────────────────────────────────────────────────────────┘
```

2. Creating a View

a. Create a temporary view named **vsched** that extracts schedule information for airline employees. **vsched** must join data from the tables **airline.staffmaster** and **airline.flightschedule**. The view must include the date, flight number, and destination (in **airline.flightschedule**), and the name and ID number of each crew member assigned to that flight (in **airline.staffmaster**). Display the view and order the report by date, flight number, and employee last name.

Partial Output

```
┌───────────────────────────────────────────────────────────────────────────────┐
│                              View VSCHED                                       │
│                                                                               │
│  Date       FlightNumber  Destination  FirstName   LastName    EmpID          │
│                                                                               │
│  01MAR2000  132           YYZ          JONATHAN    BOYCE       1739           │
│  01MAR2000  132           YYZ          SHARON      DEAN        1983           │
│  01MAR2000  132           YYZ          JAMES       NEWTON      1478           │
│  01MAR2000  132           YYZ          JEREMY      RHODES      1111           │
│  01MAR2000  132           YYZ          JONATHAN    SMART       1390           │
│  01MAR2000  132           YYZ          DEBORAH     WOOD        1130           │
│  01MAR2000  182           YYZ          FRANKLIN    CASTON      1269           │
│  01MAR2000  182           YYZ          ROGER       DENNIS      1118           │
│  01MAR2000  182           YYZ          ALAN        GOMEZ       1094           │
│  01MAR2000  182           YYZ          ALICE       MURPHY      1115           │
│  01MAR2000  182           YYZ          RANDALL     VENTER      1076           │
│  01MAR2000  182           YYZ          JOANN       YOUNG       1122           │
└───────────────────────────────────────────────────────────────────────────────┘
```

b. Use the **vsched** view to display the schedule of Deborah Young (**EmpID='1431'**). Order the report by date and flight.

```
                       Schedule for Deborah Young

Date        FlightNumber  Destination  FirstName   LastName      EmpID

01MAR2000   387           CPH          DEBORAH     YOUNG          1431
03MAR2000   622           FRA          DEBORAH     YOUNG          1431
04MAR2000   821           LHR          DEBORAH     YOUNG          1431
05MAR2000   132           YYZ          DEBORAH     YOUNG          1431
07MAR2000   821           LHR          DEBORAH     YOUNG          1431
```

c. (Optional) Use the view **vsched** and the table **airline.flightdelays** to determine how many delayed flights (**Delay>0**) each crew member was on. Order the report by employee first name and last name.

Partial Output

```
                    Number of Delayed Flights
                 Experienced by Each Crew Member

            FirstName        LastName          count

            ADAM             STEPHENSON           7
            AGNES            WELLS                6
            ALAN             GOMEZ                2
            ALICE            MURPHY               4
            ALICIA           EATON                3
            ALVIN            GRAHAM               4
            ANNA             VEGA                 3
            ANNE             PARKER               2
            ANTHONY          COOPER               3
            BARBARA          ARTHUR               1
            CAROL            PEARCE               3
            CASEY            RICHARDS             1
            CHARLES          HARRIS               4
            CHRISTINE        BRADY                2
            CLYDE            HUNTER               1
            DANIEL           GRANT                5
            DEBORAH          WOOD                 3
```

4.4 Maintaining Tables

Objectives

- Update or delete data values in an existing table.
- Add, drop, or alter the attributes of columns in a table.
- Delete tables, views, and indexes.

69

Maintaining Tables: Overview

You can use PROC SQL to do the following:

- modify values in a table or view
- add rows to a table or view
- delete rows from a table or view
- alter column attributes of a table
- add new columns to a table
- drop columns from a table
- delete an entire table, SQL view, or index

70

Updating Data Values

Use the UPDATE statement to modify column values in existing rows of a table or SAS/ACCESS view.

General form of the UPDATE statement:

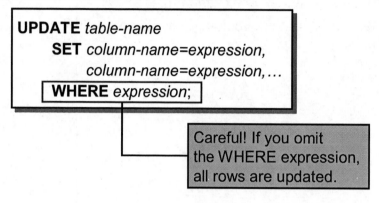

UPDATE *table-name*
    SET *column-name=expression,*
            column-name=expression, ...
    WHERE *expression;*

Careful! If you omit the WHERE expression, all rows are updated.

71

Updating Data Values

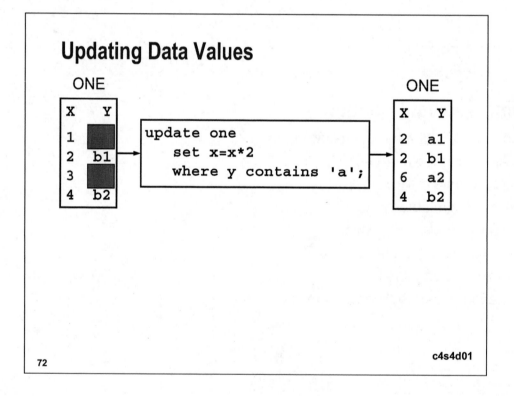

ONE

X	Y
1	▪
2	b1
3	▪
4	b2

```
update one
    set x=x*2
    where y contains 'a';
```

ONE

X	Y
2	a1
2	b1
6	a2
4	b2

72   c4s4d01

Updating Data Values

Example: Give all level 1 employees a 5% raise.

```
proc sql;
   update airline.payrollmaster
      set Salary=Salary * 1.05
      where JobCode like '__1';
   select *
      from airline.payrollmaster;
```

c4s4d02

73

A SAS DATA step equivalent is as follows:

```
data airline.payrollmaster;
   modify airline.payrollmaster;
      if substr(JobCode,3)='1' then
         Salary=Salary * 1.05;
run;
```

    You cannot create additional columns using the UPDATE statement.

Conditional Processing

Use a CASE expression to perform conditional processing. Assign new salaries based on job level. Two methods are available.

Method 1:

```
proc sql;
   update airline.payrollmaster
      set Salary=Salary *
         case substr(JobCode,3,1)
            when '1' then 1.05
            when '2' then 1.10
            when '3' then 1.15
            else 1.08
         end;
```

74   c4s4d03

A CASE expression returns a single value. It is conditionally evaluated for each row of a table or view. Use multiple WHEN clauses when you want to execute the CASE expression for some but not all rows in the table. The optional ELSE expression provides an alternate action if none of the THEN expressions is executed.

Conditional Processing

Method 2:

```
proc sql;
   update airline.payrollmaster
      set Salary=Salary *
         case when substr(JobCode,3,1)='1'
               then 1.05
               when substr(JobCode,3,1)='2'
               then 1.10
               when substr(JobCode,3,1)='3'
               then 1.15
               else 1.08
         end;
```

c4s4d04

75

Method 1 above is more efficient because the SUBSTR function is evaluated only once. This method also assumes an = comparison operator, which means that if you need a different operator, you must use Method 2.

If no ELSE expression is present and every WHEN condition is false, the result of the CASE expression is a missing value.

Conditional Processing

You can also use a CASE expression in other parts of a query, such as within a SELECT statement, to create new columns.

General form of the CASE expression within the SELECT statement:

```
SELECT column-1<, column-2> ...
    CASE <case-operand>
    WHEN when-condition THEN result-expression
    <WHEN when-condition THEN result-expression>
    <ELSE result-expression>
END <as column>
FROM table;
```

76

Conditional Processing

Example: Display employee names, job codes, and
job levels.

```
proc sql;
   select LastName, FirstName, JobCode,
          case substr(JobCode,3,1)
              when '1' then 'junior'
              when '2' then 'intermediate'
              when '3' then 'senior'
              else 'none'
          end as level
      from airline.payrollmaster,
          airline.staffmaster
      where staffmaster.EmpID=
          payrollmaster.EmpID;
```

77   c4s4d05

In traditional SAS programming language, you create a user-defined format with the FORMAT procedure
to display a character string of your choice, in place of a stored value.

Conditional Processing

Partial Output

```
                      The SAS System

                                   Job
        LastName        FirstName  Code   level

        ADAMS           GERALD     TA2    intermediate
        ALEXANDER       SUSAN      ME2    intermediate
        APPLE           TROY       ME1    junior
        ARTHUR          BARBARA    FA3    senior
        AVERY           JERRY      TA3    senior
        BAREFOOT        JOSEPH     ME3    senior
        BAUCOM          WALTER     SCP    none
        BLAIR           JUSTIN     PT2    intermediate
        BLALOCK         RALPH      TA2    intermediate
        BOSTIC          MARIE      TA3    senior
```

78

Loading Data into a Table: Review

Method A: The SET Clause

INSERT INTO *table*
    SET *column-1=value,column-2=value,...;*

Method B: The VALUES Clause

INSERT INTO *table* <*(column-list)*>
    VALUES (*value,value,value, ...*);

Method C: A Query-expression

INSERT INTO *table-1* <*(column-list)*>
    SELECT *columns* **FROM** *table-2*

79

Deleting Rows

Use the DELETE statement to eliminate unwanted rows from a a table or SAS/ACCESS view.

General form of the DELETE statement:

DELETE FROM *table*
    WHERE *expression*;

80

If you do not specify a WHERE clause, all rows are deleted.

Deleting Rows

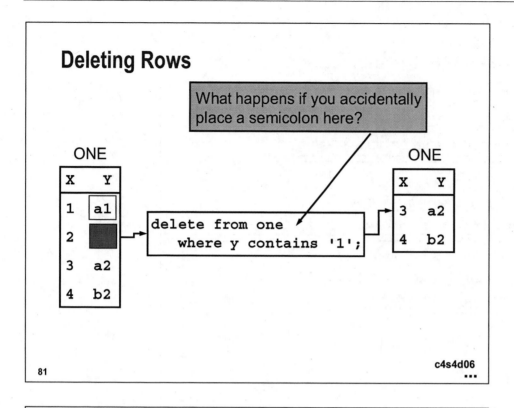

81   c4s4d06
                                                                                      ...

Deleting Rows

Example: From the **airline.frequentflyers**
          table, delete all frequent flyers who either used
          all their points or used more than they have.

```
proc sql;
   delete from airline.frequentflyers
      where PointsEarned-PointsUsed <= 0;
```

Partial Log

```
NOTE: 11 rows were deleted from AIRLINE.FREQUENTFLYERS.
```

82   c4s4d07

✎   Compare this process with the subsetting IF statement used in traditional SAS programming
     language.

Altering Columns

Use the ALTER statement to manipulate columns in a table three different ways.

General form of the ALTER statement:

```
ALTER TABLE table
    ADD column-definition, column-definition, …
    DROP column-1, column-2, …
    MODIFY column-definition, column-definition, …;
```

83

Altering Columns

1. Add columns to a table.

```
proc sql;
    alter table airline.payrollmaster
        add Bonus num format=comma10.2,
            Level char(3);
```

c4s4d08

84

After adding columns, use the UPDATE statement to assign values to those columns. These added columns initially contain missing values.

Altering Columns

2. Drop columns from a table.

```
proc sql;
   alter table airline.flightdelays
      drop DestinationType;
```

c4s4d09

85

An alternative is to use the DROP= data set option as follows:

```
create table airline.flightdelays
   select *
      from airline.flightdelays (drop=DestinationType);
```

Altering Columns

3. Modify attributes of existing columns in a table. You can alter a column's length, informat, format, and label.

```
proc sql;
   alter table airline.payrollmaster
      modify Bonus num format=comma8.2,
             Level char(1)
                label='Employee Level';
```

c4s4d10

86

Altering Columns

Example: Alter `airline.payrollmaster` as follows:

1. Add a new column named **Age**.
2. Change the **DateOfBirth** column to the MMDDYY10. format.
3. Drop the **DateOfHire** column.

Create the columns here.   Populate the rows here.

```
proc sql;
   alter table airline.payrollmaster
      add Age num
      modify DateOfBirth date format=mmddyy10.
      drop DateOfHire;
   update airline.payrollmaster
      set Age=int((today()-DateOfBirth)/365.25);
```

c4s4d11

87

Altering Columns

Before altering

EmpID	Gender	Job Code	Salary	DateOfBirth	DateOfHire
1919	M	TA2	$48,126	16SEP1958	07JUN1985
1653	F	ME2	$49,151	19OCT1962	12AUG1988
1400	M	ME1	$41,677	08NOV1965	19OCT1988

The SAS System

```
select *
   from airline.payrollmaster;
```

After altering

EmpID	Gender	Job Code	Salary	DateOfBirth	Age
1919	M	TA2	$48,126	09/16/1958	41
1653	F	ME2	$49,151	10/19/1962	37
1400	M	ME1	$41,677	11/08/1965	34

The SAS System

88

Deleting Tables, Indexes, and Views

Use the DROP statement to delete an entire table,
SQL view, or index.

General form of the DROP statement:

> **DROP TABLE** *table-1, table-2, ...;*
> **DROP VIEW** *view-1, view-2, ...;*
> **DROP INDEX** *index-1, index-2, ...*
>   **FROM** *table;*

89

Deleting Tables, Indexes, and Views

Example: Delete the index EmpID from the
         `airline.payrollmaster` table and
         delete the temporary table `Discount`.

Partial Log

```
proc sql;
   drop index EmpID
        from airline.payrollmaster;

NOTE: Index EmpID has been dropped.
   drop table Discount;

NOTE: Table WORK.DISCOUNT has been dropped.
```

c4s4d12

90

When you delete a table, all indexes on that table are automatically deleted. If you copy a table,
all indexes are copied.

In Summary

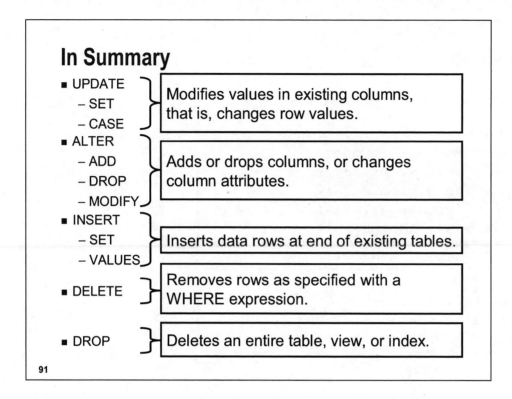

- UPDATE
  - SET
  - CASE

Modifies values in existing columns, that is, changes row values.

- ALTER
  - ADD
  - DROP
  - MODIFY

Adds or drops columns, or changes column attributes.

- INSERT
  - SET
  - VALUES

Inserts data rows at end of existing tables.

- DELETE

Removes rows as specified with a WHERE expression.

- DROP

Deletes an entire table, view, or index.

91

Updating Views

You can update the data underlying PROC SQL views using the INSERT, DELETE, and UPDATE statements, but

- you can only update a single table through a view. It cannot be joined or linked to another table, nor contain a subquery.

- you can update a column using the column's alias, but not a derived column.

- you cannot update the table through a summary query.

- you cannot update a view containing an ORDER BY clause.

92

Updating Views

Create a view...

```
proc sql;
   create view airline.raise as
       select EmpID, JobCode,
              Salary, Salary/12
              as MonthlySalary
              format=dollar12.
         from airline.payrollmaster;
```

... and then update the view.

```
proc sql;
   update airline.raise
       set Salary=Salary * 1.20
       where JobCode='PT3';
```

93   c4s4d13

Can't do stuff with monthlysalary since it is a Calculated field.

 **Exercises**

Submit a LIBNAME statement to assign **airline** to the course SAS data library.

TSO: `libname airline '.sql.sasdata';`

Directory-based systems: `libname airline '.';`

3. **Modifying a Table**

   a. Create a temporary table named **tdelay** that is a copy of the table
      airline.flightdelays, but contains only the data for March 1, 2000.

   b. Flight numbers must be modified to differentiate international flights from domestic flights.
      Change the **FlightNumber** column in the **tdelay** table from three characters to four
      characters wide.

   c. Modify the flight numbers so that international flights
      (**DestinationType='International'**) have flight numbers beginning with '**I**'.
      Domestic flight numbers remain the same. Display **tdelay**.

   d. Eliminate the **DestinationType** column from **tdelay**.

   e. Delay categories must be altered to reflect new standards. Change the values of the
      DelayCategory column as indicated below. Display the **tdelay** table.

Value of Delay	New Value of DelayCategory
0 and below	'No Delay'
1 to 15	'Acceptable'
16 and over	'Excessive'

   f. Delete the **tdelay** table.

4.5 Chapter Summary

You can use PROC SQL to create tables in several ways. You can define columns or borrow column definitions with the CREATE TABLE statement. Use an INSERT statement to enter rows of data into the table. Use the CREATE TABLE statement with an AS keyword to store the result of a query into a table.

A view is a stored query that contains no data but can be used as a table. You can create or update views using PROC SQL. You can use the DESCRIBE statement to display the definition of a PROC SQL view in the SAS log.

You can use PROC SQL to create indexes on tables. PROC SQL can use indexes to optimize the processing of WHERE clauses and joins.

PROC SQL enables you to alter or delete rows of data in existing tables or views using the UPDATE and DELETE statements, respectively. You can use the ALTER statement to add, delete, or modify the attributes of columns in an existing table. Use the DROP statement to delete tables, views, and indexes.

General form of PROC SQL using integrity constraints:

> **PROC SQL**;
>   **CREATE TABLE** *table*
>   (*column-specification,...*
>   *<constraint-specification,...>*

General forms of the CREATE TABLE statement:

> **CREATE TABLE** *table*
>   (*column-1 type(length),*
>   *column-2 type(length), ...*);

> **CREATE TABLE** *table-1*
>   **LIKE** *table-2*;

> **CREATE TABLE** *table-1* **AS**
>   **SELECT** *column-1, column-2, ...*
>   **FROM** *table-2 ...*;

General forms of the INSERT statement:

> **INSERT INTO** *table*
>   **SET** *column-1=value,*
>   *column-2=value, ...;*

> **INSERT INTO** *table*
>   **VALUES** (*value,value, ...*);

> **INSERT INTO** *table-1*
>   **SELECT** *column-1, column-2, ...*
>   **FROM** *table-2 ...;*

General form of the CREATE VIEW statement:

> **CREATE VIEW** *view-nam*e **AS**
>   *query-expression*;

General form of the DESCRIBE statement:

> **DESCRIBE VIEW** *view-name*;

General form of the CREATE INDEX statement:

> **CREATE <UNIQUE> INDEX** *index-name*
>   **ON** *table(column-1,column-2)*;

General form of the UPDATE statement:

> **UPDATE** *table | view*
>   **SET** *column-1 expression,*
>   *column-2=expression, ...*
>   **WHERE** *expression*;

General form of the CASE expression within the SELECT statement:

> **SELECT** *column-1<, column-2> ...*
>   **CASE** *<case-operand>*
>   **WHEN** *when-condition* **THEN** *result-expression*
>   **<WHEN** *when-condition* **THEN** *result-expression>*
>   **<ELSE** *result-expression>*
> **END**;

General form of the DELETE statement:

> **DELETE FROM** *table*
>   **WHERE** *expression*;

General form of the ALTER statement:

ALTER TABLE *table*
    ADD *column-definition, column-definition, …*
    DROP *column-1, column-2, …;*
    MODIFY *column-definition, column-definition, …*

General forms of the DROP statement:

DROP TABLE *table-1, table-2, …;*
DROP *view-1, view-2, …;*
DROP INDEX *index-1, index-2, …***FROM** *table*;

4.6 Solutions to Exercises

1. Creating a Table

a.

```
proc sql;
   create table awards
      (ptsreqd num label='Points Required',
      rank num format=3.,
      award char(25));
```

b.

```
insert into awards
   values( 2000, 1, 'free night in hotel')
   values(10000, 2, '50% discount on flight')
   values(20000, 3, 'free domestic flight')
   values(40000, 4, 'free international flight');
```

Alternate Solution

```
insert into awards
   set ptsreqd=2000, rank=1,
      award='free night in hotel'
   set ptsreqd=10000, rank=2,
      award='50% discount on flight'
   set ptsreqd=20000, rank=3,
      award='free domestic flight'
   set ptsreqd=40000, rank=4,
      award='free international flight';
```

c.

```
select *
   from awards;
```

d.

```
title 'Awards Available to AZ Frequent Flyers';
   select FFID,Name,
      PointsEarned-PointsUsed
      label='Available Points',
      award
      from airline.frequentflyers,awards
      where (PointsEarned-PointsUsed)>=ptsreqd
      and State='AZ'
      order by 1;
```

e. (Optional)

```
title 'Frequent Flyers Ineligible for Awards';
   select distinct FFID, Name,
           PointsEarned-PointsUsed
           label='Available Points'
      from airline.frequentflyers
      where (PointsEarned-PointsUsed)<all
         (select ptsreqd
             from awards)
      order by 1;
quit;
title;
```

2. Creating a View

a.

```
proc sql;
   create view vsched as
      select Date, FlightNumber,
              flightschedule.Destination,
              FirstName, LastName, staffmaster.EmpID
          from airline.staffmaster, airline.flightschedule
          where staffmaster.EmpID=flightschedule.EmpID;
title 'View VSCHED';
   select *
      from vsched
      order by Date, FlightNumber, LastName;
```

b.

```
title 'Schedule for Deborah Young';
   select *
      from vsched
      where EmpID='1431'
      order by Date, FlightNumber;
```

c. (Optional)

```
title 'Number of Delayed Flights';
title2 'Experienced by Each Crew Member';
   select FirstName, LastName,
           count(*) as count
      from vsched, airline.flightdelays
      where vsched.FlightNumber=flightdelays.FlightNumber
           and vsched.Date=FlightDelays.Date
           and Delay>0
      group by FirstName, LastName
      order by FirstName, LastName;
quit;
title;
```

3. Modifying a Table

a.

```
proc sql;
   create table tdelay as
      select *
         from airline.flightdelays
         where Date='01mar2000'd;
```

b.

```
alter table tdelay
   modify FlightNumber char(4);
```

c.

```
update tdelay
   set FlightNumber='I'||FlightNumber
   where DestinationType='International';
select *
   from tdelay;
```

d.

```
alter table tdelay
   drop DestinationType;
```

e.

```
update tdelay
   set DelayCategory=
      case
         when Delay<=0 then 'No Delay'
         when 0<Delay<=15 then 'Acceptable'
         else 'Excessive'
      end;
select *
   from tdelay;
```

f.

```
drop table tdelay;
quit;
```

Chapter 5   Additional SQL Features

5.1   Setting SQL Procedure Options

Objectives

- Use SQL procedure options to control processing details.
- Reset PROC SQL options without re-invoking the procedure.

3

Controlling Processing

The SQL procedure offers a variety of options and statements that affect processing.

General form of the PROC SQL statement:

PROC SQL *options*;

4

Controlling Processing

Selected options:

INOBS=*n*   sets a limit of *n* rows from each source table that contributes to a query.

OUTOBS=*n* restricts the number of rows that a query outputs (displays or writes to a table).

continued...

5

Controlling Processing

PRINT|NOPRINT   controls whether the results of a SELECT statement are displayed.

NONUMBER|NUMBER   controls whether the row number is printed as the first column in the output.

NODOUBLE|DOUBLE   double-spaces the report.

continued...

6

The default value appears first in the slides.

Controlling Processing

NOFLOW|FLOW| controls the appearance of
FLOW=*n*|FLOW=*n m*   wide character columns. The
                              FLOW option causes text to be
                              flowed in its column rather than
                              wrapping the entire row.
                              Specifying *n* determines the
                              width of the flowed column.
                              Specifying *n* and *m* floats the
                              width of the column between
                              the limits to achieve a balanced
                              layout.

7

Controlling Processing

Example: Display the AWARDS table with flowed
          character columns and double-spacing.

```
proc sql flow=13 double;
   select *
      from awards;
```

8   c5s1d01

Controlling Processing

Output

```
Points
Required      Rank  Award

   2000          1  free night
                    in hotel

  10000          2  50% discount
                    on flight

  20000          3  free domestic
                    flight

  40000          4  free
                    international
                    flight
```

9

Controlling Processing

Example: Read ten rows from
          airline.marchflights.

```
proc sql inobs=10;
   select FlightNumber, Date
      from airline.marchflights;
```

10

c5s1d02

Controlling Processing

Output

FlightNumber	Date
182	01MAR2000
114	01MAR2000
202	01MAR2000
219	01MAR2000
439	01MAR2000
387	01MAR2000
290	01MAR2000
523	01MAR2000
982	01MAR2000
622	01MAR2000

11

After you specify an option, it remains in effect until you change it or you re-invoke PROC SQL.

Resetting Options

You can use the RESET statement to add or change PROC SQL options without re-invoking the procedure.

General form of the RESET statement:

RESET *options*;

12

Resetting Options

Example: Display two rows from the payroll table and
print the row number. Then display the rows
without printing the row number.

```
proc sql outobs=2 number;
   select * from airline.payrollmaster;
```

Output

Row	Emp ID	Gender	Job Code	Salary	DateOfBirth	DateOfHire
1	1919	M	TA2	$48,126	16SEP1958	07JUN1985
2	1653	F	ME2	$49,151	19OCT1962	12AUG1988

c5s1d03

13

Resetting Options

```
reset nonumber;
select *
from airline.payrollmaster;
```

Output

Emp ID	Gender	Job Code	Salary	DateOfBirth	DateOfHire
1919	M	TA2	$48,126	16SEP1958	07JUN1985
1653	F	ME2	$49,151	19OCT1962	12AUG1988

c5s1d04

14

5.2 Dictionary Tables and Views

Objectives

- Use dictionary tables and views to obtain information about SAS files.

16

Overview

You can retrieve information about SAS session metadata by querying *dictionary tables* with PROC SQL. Dictionary tables follow these rules:

- created at initialization
- updated automatically
- limited to read-only access

data about data (metadata)

17

"Metadata consist of information that characterizes data. Metadata are used to provide documentation for data products. In essence, metadata answer **who, what, when, where, why,** and **how** about every facet of the data that are being documented."

http://geology.usgs.gov/tools/metadata/tools/doc/faq.html#motivation

Overview

The metadata available in dictionary tables includes the following:

- SAS files
- external files
- system options, macros, titles, and footnotes

18

Overview of SAS File Metadata

`DICTIONARY.MEMBERS`

  – general information about data library members

`DICTIONARY.TABLES`

  – detailed information about data sets

`DICTIONARY.COLUMNS`

  – detailed information on variables and their attributes

`DICTIONARY.CATALOGS`

  – information about catalog entries

`DICTIONARY.VIEWS`

  – general information about data views

`DICTIONARY.INDEXES`

  – information on indexes defined for data files

continued...

19

Overview of SAS File Metadata

`DICTIONARY.CHECK_CONSTRAINTS`

- information about known check constraints

`DICTIONARY.CONSTRAINT_COLUMN_USAGE`

- information about columns that are referred to by integrity constraints

`DICTIONARY.CONSTRAINT_TABLE_USAGE`

- information about tables that have integrity constraints defined on them

`DICTIONARY.TABLE_CONSTRAINTS`

- information about integrity constraints in all known tables

`DICTIONARY.REFERENTIAL_CONSTRAINTS`

- information about referential constraints

20

Overview of Other Metadata

`DICTIONARY.EXTFILES`

- information about currently assigned filerefs

`DICTIONARY.OPTIONS`

- information about current settings of SAS system options

`DICTIONARY.MACROS`

- information about macro variables

`DICTIONARY.TITLES`

- information about text assigned to titles and footnotes

21

SAS librefs are limited to eight characters. DICTIONARY is an automatically assigned, reserved word.

Exploring Dictionary Tables

```
describe table dictionary.tables;
```

Partial Log

```
NOTE: SQL table DICTIONARY.TABLES was created like:

create table DICTIONARY.TABLES
   (
   libname char(8) label='Library Name',
   memname char(32) label='Member Name',
   memtype char(8) label='Member Type',
   dbms_memtype char(32) label='DBMS Member Type',
   memlabel char(256) label='Dataset Label',
   typemem char(8) label='Dataset Type',
   crdate num format=DATETIME informat=DATETIME label='Date Created',
   modate num format=DATETIME informat=DATETIME label='Date Modified',
   nobs num label='Number of Observations',
   obslen num label='Observation Length',
   nvar num label='Number of Variables', ...);
```

22

c5s2d01

The DESCRIBE TABLE statement is a good tool for exploring dictionary tables. The complete log notes from the DESCRIBE statement are shown below:

```
create table DICTIONARY.TABLES
  (
   libname char(8) label='Library Name',
   memname char(32) label='Member Name',
   memtype char(8) label='Member Type',
   dbms_memtype char(32) label='DBMS Member Type',
   memlabel char(256) label='Dataset Label',
   typemem char(8) label='Dataset Type',
   crdate num format=DATETIME informat=DATETIME label='Date Created',
   modate num format=DATETIME informat=DATETIME label='Date Modified',
   nobs num label='Number of Physical Observations',
   obslen num label='Observation Length',
   nvar num label='Number of Variables',
   protect char(3) label='Type of Password Protection',
   compress char(8) label='Compression Routine',
   encrypt char(8) label='Encryption',
   npage num label='Number of Pages',
   filesize num label='Size of File',
   pcompress num label='Percent Compression',
   reuse char(3) label='Reuse Space',
   bufsize num label='Bufsize',
   delobs num label='Number of Deleted Observations',
   nlobs num label='Number of Logical Observations',
   maxvar num label='Longest variable name',
   maxlabel num label='Longest label',
   maxgen num label='Maximum number of generations',
   gen num label='Generation number',
   attr char(3) label='Dataset Attributes',
   indxtype char(9) label='Type of Indexes',
   datarep char(32) label='Data Representation',
   sortname char(8) label='Name of Collating Sequence',
   sorttype char(4) label='Sorting Type',
   sortchar char(8) label='Charset Sorted By',
   reqvector char(24) format=$HEX48 informat=$HEX48 label='Requirements Vector',
   datarepname char(170) label='Data Representation Name',
   encoding char(256) label='Data Encoding',
   audit char(3) label='Audit Trail Active?',
   audit_before char(3) label='Audit Before Image?',
   audit_admin char(3) label='Audit Admin Image?',
   audit_error char(3) label='Audit Error Image?',
   audit_data char(3) label='Audit Data Image?'
  );
```

Using Dictionary Information

Example: Display information about the files in the
          airline library.

```
options nolabel nocenter;
proc sql;
select memname format=$20.,nobs,nvar,crdate
   from dictionary.tables
   where libname='AIRLINE';
```

23   c5s2d02

Using Dictionary Information

Output

memname	nobs	nvar	crdate
FAVIEW	.	6	15SEP06:20:15:59
FLIGHTDELAYS	624	8	18MAR00:20:53:16
FLIGHTSCHEDULE	270	4	18MAR00:20:53:17
FREQUENTFLYERS	206	11	02NOV01:09:12:41
INTERNATIONALFLIGHTS	201	4	18MAR00:20:53:16
MARCHFLIGHTS	635	13	18MAR00:20:53:16
MECHANICSLEVEL1	8	3	18MAR00:20:53:17
MECHANICSLEVEL2	14	3	18MAR00:20:53:17
MECHANICSLEVEL3	7	3	18MAR00:20:53:17
PAYROLLCHANGES	6	6	18MAR00:20:53:17
PAYROLLMASTER	148	6	18MAR00:20:53:17
PAYROLLMASTER2	148	6	21JAN04:13:33:35
STAFFCHANGES	6	6	18MAR00:20:53:18
STAFFMASTER	148	6	18MAR00:20:53:17
SUPERVISORS	19	3	18MAR00:20:53:18

24

Using Dictionary Information

Example: Determine which tables contain the EmpID
column.

```
select memname
  from dictionary.columns
  where libname='AIRLINE' and name='EmpID';
```

c5s2d03

25

Using Dictionary Information

Output

```
memname
_____
FLIGHTSCHEDULE
MECHANICSLEVEL1
MECHANICSLEVEL2
MECHANICSLEVEL3
PAYROLLCHANGES
PAYROLLMASTER
STAFFCHANGES
STAFFMASTER
SUPERVISORS
```

26

Using Dictionary Information

To use session metadata in other procedures or in a
DATA step, you can do the following:

- create a PROC SQL view based on a dictionary table
- use views provided in the SASHELP library that are
  based on the dictionary tables

27

Using Dictionary Information

Example: Use **sashelp.vmember** to extract
information from DICTIONARY.MEMBERS
in a PROC TABULATE step.

```
proc tabulate data=sashelp.vmember format=8.;
   class libname memtype;
   keylabel N=' ';
   table libname, memtype/rts=10
      misstext='None';
run;
```

28

c5s2d04

Using Dictionary Information

Output

	Member Type				
	CATALOG	DATA	ITEMSTOR	MDDB	VIEW
Library Name					
AIRLINE	None	14	None	None	1
SASHELP	101	91	2	2	30
SASUSER	5	106	1	None	4
SQL	None	14	None	None	1
WORK	None	2	None	None	1

29

5.3   Interfacing PROC SQL with Macro Language (Optional)

Objectives

- Create and use SAS macro variables in PROC SQL.
- Understand the use of SAS macros with SQL processing.
- Use the automatic SAS macro variables created by PROC SQL.

31

Resolving Symbolic References

Macro variable references embedded within PROC SQL code are resolved as the source code is tokenized.

This sounds familiar!

32

Resolving Symbolic References

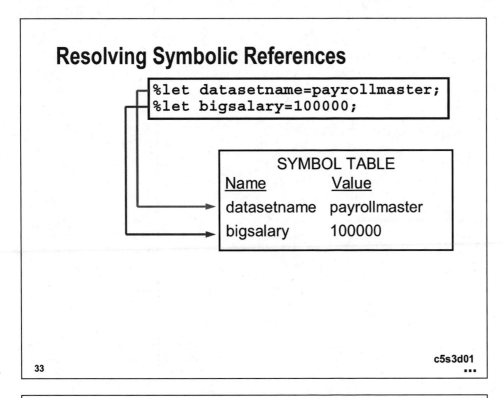

```
%let datasetname=payrollmaster;
%let bigsalary=100000;
```

SYMBOL TABLE

Name	Value
datasetname	payrollmaster
bigsalary	100000

33   c5s3d01
...

Resolving Symbolic References

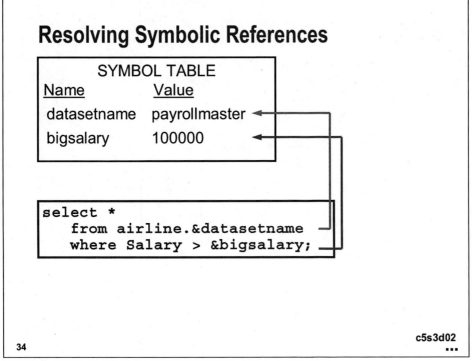

SYMBOL TABLE

Name	Value
datasetname	payrollmaster
bigsalary	100000

```
select *
   from airline.&datasetname
   where Salary > &bigsalary;
```

34   c5s3d02
...

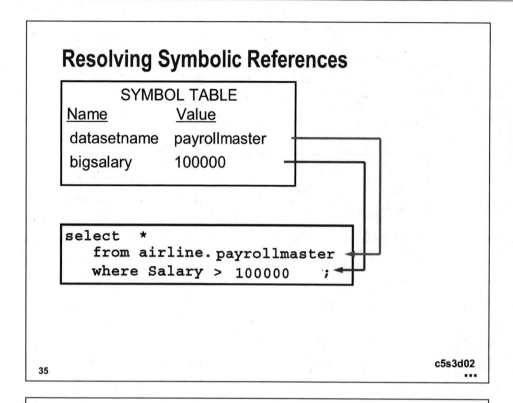

Resolving Symbolic References

SYMBOL TABLE

Name	Value
datasetname	payrollmaster
bigsalary	100000

```
select  *
   from airline. payrollmaster
   where Salary > 100000    ;
```

35   c5s3d02
                                                           ...

Creating Macro Variables

- SQL enables a query to pass data values to variables in the host software system. SAS chose to implement these host variables as macro variables.
- PROC SQL can create or update macro variables using an INTO clause. This clause can be used in three ways.

36

PROC SQL can create or update macro variables in either local or global symbol tables.

The INTO clause occurs between the SELECT and FROM clauses. It cannot be used in a CREATE TABLE or CREATE VIEW statement. Use the NOPRINT option if you do not need a display of the query result.

Creating Macro Variables: Method 1

General form of the SELECT statement with an INTO keyword:

SELECT *column-1, column-2, ...*
    INTO *:macro-var-1, :macro-var-2, ...*
    FROM ...

Method 1 extracts values **only** from the **first** row of the query result.

37

This method is often used with queries that return only one row.

Creating Macro Variables: Method 1

```
reset noprint;
select avg(Salary),
       min(Salary),
       max(Salary)
   into :mean, :min, :max
   from airline.payrollmaster;
%put &mean &min &max;
```

Partial Log

```
54079.65   25120.2 155930.6
```

c5s3d03

38

Creating Macro Variables: Method 1

Calculate the average salary of employees with a
particular job code. Store the average in a macro variable
and use the average to display all employees in that job
code who have a salary above the average. Place the
average in a title.

39

Creating Macro Variables: Method 1

```
%let code=NA1;
proc sql noprint;
select avg(Salary) into :mean
    from airline.payrollmaster
    where JobCode="&code";

reset print;

title1 "&code Employees Earning Above-"
       "Average Salaries";
title2 "Average Salary for &code Employees "
       "Is &mean";
select *
    from airline.payrollmaster
    where Salary > &mean and JobCode="&code";
```

40   c5s3d04

% sysfunc (putn(&mean. , dollar10. 2))

↓
data step
fns. outside
    data step

Creating Macro Variables: Method 1

Output

```
      NA1 Employees Earning Above-Average Salaries
      Average Salary for NA1 Employees Is 58845.08

                    Job
   EmpID Gender    Code    Salary    DateOfBirth  DateOfHire

   1839    F       NA1    $60,806     02DEC1968    07JUL1991
   1332    M       NA1    $59,049     20SEP1968    07JUN1989
   1443    F       NA1    $59,184     21NOV1966    01SEP1989
```

41

Creating Macro Variables: Method 2

General form of the SELECT statement to create a macro variable:

```
SELECT a, b, ...
     INTO :a1-:an, :b1-:bn
     FROM ...
```

Method 2 extracts values from the first *n* rows of the query result and puts them into a series of *n* macro variables.

42

Creating Macro Variables: Method 2

How many frequent flyers are in each of the three member types (GOLD, SILVER, BRONZE)?

```
reset noprint;
select MemberType,
        count(*) as Frequency
    into :memtype1-:memtype3,:freq1-:freq3
    from airline.frequentflyers
    group by MemberType;
```

43   c5s3d05

Creating Macro Variables: Method 2

Example

```
%put Member types: &memtype1 &memtype2 &memtype3;
%put Frequencies: &freq1 &freq2 &freq3;
```

Partial Log

```
Member types: BRONZE GOLD SILVER
Frequencies: 61 60 85
```

44   c5s3d06

Creating Macro Variables: Method 3

General form of the SELECT statement to create a macro variable:

SELECT *column-1, column-2, ...*
    INTO *:macro-var-1* **SEPARATED BY** *'delimiter'* ,
        :macro-var-2 **SEPARATED BY** *'delimiter'* ...
    FROM ...

Method 3 extracts values from all rows of the query result and puts them into a single macro variable, separated by the specified delimiter.

45

Creating Macro Variables: Method 3

Put the unique values of all international destinations into a single macro variable.

```
select distinct Destination
    into :airportcodes
        separated by ' '
    from airline.internationalflights;
%put &airportcodes;
```

Partial Log

```
CDG CPH FRA LHR YYZ
```

c5s3d07

46

The long string value in the macro variable can be parsed into the individual short values using %SCAN.

Automatic Macro Variables

Execution of a PROC SQL query or non-query statement updates the following automatic macro variables:

SQLOBS   records the number of rows output or deleted.

SQLRC   contains the return code from each SQL statement.

SQLOOPS   contains the number of iterations processed by the inner loop of PROC SQL.

ignore SQLOOPS

47

Automatic Macro Variables

Write a macro that accepts a state code as a parameter and creates a table containing employees from that state. Display a maximum of ten rows from the table.

48

Automatic Macro Variables

```
%macro state(st);
proc sql;
create table &st as
select LastName, FirstName
   from airline.staffmaster
   where State="&st";
%put NOTE: The table &st has &sqlobs rows.;
title1 "&st Employees";
%if &sqlobs > 10 %then %do;
%put
   NOTE: Only the first 10 rows are displayed.;
   title2 "NOTE: Only 10 rows are displayed.";
   reset outobs=10;
%end;
select * from &st;
quit;
%mend state;
```

49   c5s3d08

Automatic Macro Variables

```
%state(NY)
```

Partial Log

```
NOTE: Table WORK.NY created, with 89 rows and 2 columns.

NOTE: The table NY has 89 rows.
NOTE: Only the first 10 rows are displayed.
WARNING: Statement terminated early due to OUTOBS=10 option.
```

50   c5s3d09

Automatic Macro Variables

Output

```
                  NY Employees
        NOTE: Only 10 rows are displayed.

        LastName          FirstName
        _____

        APPLE             TROY
        ARTHUR            BARBARA
        BAUCOM            WALTER
        BLALOCK           RALPH
        BOSTIC            MARIE
        BOYCE             JONATHAN
        BRADLEY           JEREMY
        BRYANT            LEONARD
        BURNETTE          THOMAS
        CAHILL            MARSHALL
```

51

5.4 Program Testing and Performance

Objectives

- Use PROC SQL options to test SQL code.
- Understand SAS log messages and accurately benchmark SAS code.

53

Testing and Performance Options

PROC SQL statement options are available to aid
in testing programs and evaluating performance.

The following are selected options:

- EXEC|NOEXEC controls whether submitted SQL
  statements are executed.
- NOSTIMER|STIMER reports performance statistics
  in the SAS log for each SQL statement.
- NOERRORSTOP|ERRORSTOP is used in batch
  and noninteractive jobs to make PROC SQL enter
  syntax-check mode after an error occurs.

54

To use the STIMER SQL option, the system option STIMER or FULLSTIMER must also be in
effect.

Other PROC SQL statement options that are useful in testing include

- INOBS=*n*
- OUTOBS=*n*.

Testing and Performance Options

Display the columns that are retrieved when you use
SELECT * in a query and display any macro variable
resolutions, but do not execute the query.

```
%let datasetname=payrollmaster;

proc sql feedback noexec;
    select *
        from airline.&datasetname;
```

c5s4d01

55

Testing and Performance Options

Partial Log

→ Comes from feedback option (handwritten)

```
NOTE: Statement transforms to:
select PAYROLLMASTER.EmpID, PAYROLLMASTER.Gender,
PAYROLLMASTER.JobCode,
PAYROLLMASTER.Salary, PAYROLLMASTER.DateOfBirth,
PAYROLLMASTER.DateOfHire
        from AIRLINE.PAYROLLMASTER;


NOTE: Statement not executed due to NOEXEC option.
```

56

Testing and Performance Options

This is a log from a PROC SQL step with the STIMER
statement option that executes a single query. The first
note concerns the invocation of PROC SQL:

```
NOTE: The SQL statement used the following resources:
      CPU     time -         00:00:00.01
      Elapsed time -         00:00:00.68
      EXCP count   - 28
      Task memory  - 110K (20K data, 90K program)
      Total memory - 864K (760K data, 104K program)
```

→ wall clock time depends on other things going on. (handwritten)

The second note concerns the query itself.

```
NOTE: The SQL statement used the following resources:
      CPU     time -         00:00:00.23
      Elapsed time -         00:00:03.61
      EXCP count   - 157
      Task  memory - 1213K (828K data, 385K program)
      Total memory - 2258K (1840K data, 418K program)
```

57

This program was run in batch under z/OS. Performance measures, as well as the actual numbers,
vary greatly across installations and operating systems. (The query used is the one about the
supervisors of the crew on the Copenhagen flight, using subqueries and in-line views, from
Section 3.3.)

Testing and Performance Options

Example

The third note reflects the totals for the procedure.

```
NOTE: The SQL procedure used the following resources:
      CPU     time -           00:00:00.25
      Elapsed time -           00:00:04.34
      EXCP count   - 186
      Task  memory - 1213K (828K data, 385K program)
      Total memory - 2258K (1840K data, 418K program)
```

58

General Guidelines for Benchmarking Programs

- Never use elapsed time for comparison because it might be affected by concurrent tasks.
- Benchmark two programs in separate SAS sessions. If benchmarking is done within one SAS session, statistics for the second program can be misleading because the SAS supervisor might have loaded modules into memory from prior steps.

59

General Guidelines for Benchmarking Programs

- Run each program multiple times and average the performance statistics.
- Use realistic data for tests. Program A could be better than program B on small tables and worse on large tables.

60

5.5 Chapter Summary

You can use options in the PROC SQL statement to affect SQL processing. You can limit the number of rows read or written during a query or limit the number of internal loops PROC SQL performs. PROC SQL can notify you when any of the processing limits that you set are reaches.

Options are also available that affect the form of the output. You can flow character columns, number your rows, or double-space output. The RESET statement enables you to change options without having to re-invoke the procedure.

Dictionary tables can be queried to display SAS session metadata. The dictionary tables are generated at run time and are read-only. You can also use views stored in the SASHELP library that are based on the dictionary tables.

You can combine the SAS macro facility with PROC SQL in the same way as any other SAS step. PROC SQL, however, is capable of passing data from a query result into a macro variable. PROC SQL also updates several automatic macro variables that contain information about the last query executed.

There are PROC SQL statement options available to test and evaluate program performance. For example, the STIMER option in the PROC SQL statement can request resource usage information on each statement executed. The SAS log displays information on CPU usage, I/O counts, and other statistics.

General form of the PROC SQL statement:

PROC SQL *options*;

General form of the RESET statement:

RESET *options*;

General forms of the SELECT statement with an INTO keyword:

```
SELECT column-1, column-2, ...
    INTO :macro-var-1, :macro-var-2, ...
    FROM ...

SELECT a, b, ...
    INTO :a1-:an, :b1-:bn
    FROM     ...

SELECT column-1, column-2, ...
    INTO :macro-var-1   SEPARATED BY 'delimiter'
    FROM ...
```

Macro variables created by PROC SQL:

    &SQLOBS

    &SQLRC

    &SQLOOPS

Selected PROC SQL statement options:

    INOBS=*n*

    OUTOBS= *n*

    PRINT|NOPRINT

    NONUMBER|NUMBER

    NODOUBLE|DOUBLE

    NOFLOW|FLOW|FLOW=*n*|FLOW=*n m*

    EXEC|NOEXEC

    NOSTIMER|STIMER

    NOERRORSTOP|ERRORSTOP

Appendix A Overview of Table and Column Names

A.1 Table and Column Names Sorted by Column Names

Column Name	Table Names
Address	FREQUENTFLYERS
Boarded	INTERNATIONALFLIGHTS MARCHFLIGHTS
City	FREQUENTFLYERS STAFFCHANGES STAFFMASTER
Date	FLIGHTDELAYS FLIGHTSCHEDULE INTERNATIONALFLIGHTS MARCHFLIGHTS
DateOfBirth	PAYROLLCHANGES PAYROLLMASTER
DateOfHire	PAYROLLCHANGES PAYROLLMASTER
DayOfWeek	FLIGHTDELAYS
Delay	FLIGHTDELAYS
DelayCategory	FLIGHTDELAYS
DepartureTime	MARCHFLIGHTS
Deplaned	MARCHFLIGHTS
Destination	FLIGHTDELAYS FLIGHTSCHEDULE INTERNATIONALFLIGHTS MARCHFLIGHTS
DestinationType	FLIGHTDELAYS
Distance	MARCHFLIGHTS
EmpID	FLIGHTSCHEDULE MECHANICSLEVEL1 MECHANICSLEVEL2 MECHANICSLEVEL3 PAYROLLCHANGES PAYROLLMASTER STAFFCHANGES STAFFMASTER SUPERVISORS

Column Name	Table Names
FFID	FREQUENTFLYERS
FirstName	STAFFCHANGES
	STAFFMASTER
FlightNumber	FLIGHTDELAYS
	FLIGHTSCHEDULE
	INTERNATIONALFLIGHTS
	MARCHFLIGHTS
Freight	MARCHFLIGHTS
Gender	PAYROLLCHANGES
	PAYROLLMASTER
JobCategory	SUPERVISORS
JobCode	MECHANICSLEVEL1
	MECHANICSLEVEL2
	MECHANICSLEVEL3
	PAYROLLCHANGES
	PAYROLLMASTER
LastName	STAFFCHANGES
	STAFFMASTER
Mail	MARCHFLIGHTS
MemberType	FREQUENTFLYERS
MilesTraveled	FREQUENTFLYERS
Name	FREQUENTFLYERS
Nonrevenue	MARCHFLIGHTS
Origin	FLIGHTDELAYS
	MARCHFLIGHTS
PassengerCapacity	MARCHFLIGHTS
PhoneNumber	FREQUENTFLYERS
	STAFFCHANGES
	STAFFMASTER
PointsEarned	FREQUENTFLYERS
PointsUsed	FREQUENTFLYERS
Salary	MECHANICSLEVEL1
	MECHANICSLEVEL2
	MECHANICSLEVEL3
	PAYROLLCHANGES
	PAYROLLMASTER

Column Name	Table Names
State	FREQUENTFLYERS
	STAFFCHANGES
	STAFFMASTER
	SUPERVISORS
Transferred	MARCHFLIGHTS
ZipCode	FREQUENTFLYERS

Appendix B Overview of Table and Column Names

B.1 Table and Column Names Sorted by Table Name

Table Name	Column Name	Column Type	Column Length	Column Format
FLIGHTDELAYS	FlightNumber	char	3	
	Date	num	8	DATE9.
	Origin	char	3	
	Destination	char	3	
	DelayCategory	char	15	
	DestinationType	char	15	
	DayOfWeek	num	8	
	Delay	num	8	
FLIGHTSCHEDULE	FlightNumber	char	3	$3.
	Date	num	8	DATE9.
	Destination	char	3	$3.
	EmpID	char	4	
FREQUENTFLYERS	FFID	char	6	
	MemberType	char	6	
	Name	char	25	$18.
	Address	char	20	
	PhoneNumber	char	12	
	City	char	20	$20.
	State	char	2	$2.
	ZipCode	char	5	$5.
	MilesTraveled	num	8	10.
	PointsEarned	num	8	10.
	PointsUsed	num	8	10.
INTERNATIONALFLIGHTS	FlightNumber	char	3	
	Date	num	8	DATE9.
	Destination	char	3	
	Boarded	num	8	

Table Name	Column Name	Column Type	Column Length	Column Format
MARCHFLIGHTS	FlightNumber	char	3	
	Date	num	8	DATE9.
	DepartureTime	num	8	TIME5.
	Origin	char	3	
	Destination	char	3	
	Distance	num	8	
	Mail	num	8	
	Freight	num	8	
	Boarded	num	8	
	Transferred	num	8	
	Nonrevenue	num	8	
	Deplaned	num	8	
	PassengerCapacity	num	8	
MECHANICSLEVEL1	EmpID	char	4	
	JobCode	char	3	
	Salary	num	8	DOLLAR9.
MECHANICSLEVEL2	EmpID	char	4	
	JobCode	char	3	
	Salary	num	8	DOLLAR9.
MECHANICSLEVEL3	EmpID	char	4	
	JobCode	char	3	
	Salary	num	8	DOLLAR9.
PAYROLLCHANGES	EmpID	char	4	
	Gender	char	1	
	JobCode	char	3	
	Salary	num	8	DOLLAR9.
	DateOfBirth	num	8	DATE9.
	DateOfHire	num	8	DATE9.
PAYROLLMASTER	EmpID	char	4	
	Gender	char	1	
	JobCode	char	3	
	Salary	num	8	DOLLAR9.
	DateOfBirth	num	8	DATE9.
	DateOfHire	num	8	DATE9.

Table Name	Column Name	Column Type	Column Length	Column Format
STAFFCHANGES	EmpID	char	4	
	LastName	char	15	
	FirstName	char	15	
	City	char	15	
	State	char	2	
	PhoneNumber	char	12	
STAFFMASTER	EmpID	char	4	
	LastName	char	15	
	FirstName	char	15	
	City	char	15	
	State	char	2	
	PhoneNumber	char	12	
SUPERVISORS	EmpID	char	4	
	State	char	2	
	JobCategory	char	2	

Appendix C Table Listings

C.1 Partial Table Listings

AIRLINE.FLIGHTDELAYS Table

Flight Number	Date	Origin	Destination	Delay Category	Destination Type	Day Of Week	Delay
182	01MAR2000	LGA	YYZ	No Delay	International	4	0
114	01MAR2000	LGA	LAX	1-10 Minutes	Domestic	4	8
202	01MAR2000	LGA	ORD	No Delay	Domestic	4	-5
219	01MAR2000	LGA	LHR	11+ Minutes	International	4	18
439	01MAR2000	LGA	LAX	No Delay	Domestic	4	-4

AIRLINE.FLIGHTSCHEDULE Table

Flight Number	Date	Destination	Emp. ID
132	01MAR2000	YYZ	1739
132	01MAR2000	YYZ	1478
132	01MAR2000	YYZ	1130
132	01MAR2000	YYZ	1390
132	01MAR2000	YYZ	1983

AIRLINE.FREQUENTFLYERS Table

FFID	Member Type	Name	Address	PhoneNumber
WD7152	BRONZE	COOPER, LESLIE	66 DRIVING WAY	501/377-0703
WD8472	BRONZE	LONG, RUSSELL	9813 SUMTER SQUARE	501/367-1097
WD1576	GOLD	BRYANT, ALTON	763 THISTLE DRIVE	501/776-0631
WD3947	SILVER	NORRIS, DIANE	77 PARKWAY PLAZA	501/377-3739
WD9347	SILVER	PEARSON, BRYAN	9999 MARKUP MANOR	501/855-4780

City	State	Zip Code	Miles Traveled	Points Earned	PointsUsed
Little Rock	AR	72201	30833	31333	0
Monticello	AR	71655	25570	26070	0
Bauxite	AR	72011	56144	58644	27000
North Little Rock	AR	72119	40922	45922	23000
Bella Vista	AR	72714	4839	9839	0

AIRLINE.INTERNATIONALFLIGHTS Table

Flight Number	Date	Destination	Boarded
182	01MAR2000	YYZ	104
219	01MAR2000	LHR	198
387	01MAR2000	CPH	152
622	01MAR2000	FRA	207
821	01MAR2000	LHR	205

AIRLINE.MARCHFLIGHTS Table

Flight Number	Date	Departure Time	Origin	Destination	Distance	FMail	Boarded	Transferred	Nonrevenue	Deplaned	Passenger Capacity
182	01MAR2000	8:21	LGA	YYZ	366	458	390	104	16	3	123	178
114	01MAR2000	7:10	LGA	LAX	2475	357	390	172	18	6	196	210
202	01MAR2000	10:43	LGA	ORD	740	369	244	151	11	5	157	210
219	01MAR2000	9:31	LGA	LHR	3442	412	334	198	17	7	222	250
439	01MAR2000	12:16	LGA	LAX	2475	422	267	167	13	5	185	210

AIRLINE.MECHANICSLEVEL1 Table

Emp ID	Job Code	Salary
1400	ME1	$41,677
1403	ME1	$39,301
1120	ME1	$40,067
1121	ME1	$40,757
1412	ME1	$38,919

```
                        AIRLINE.MECHANICSLEVEL2 Table

                    Emp       Job
                     ID       Code      Salary

                    1653      ME2       $49,151
                    1782      ME2       $49,483
                    1244      ME2       $51,695
                    1065      ME2       $49,126
                    1129      ME2       $48,901
```

```
                        AIRLINE.MECHANICSLEVEL3 Table

                    Emp       Job
                     ID       Code      Salary

                    1499      ME3       $60,235
                    1409      ME3       $58,171
                    1379      ME3       $59,170
                    1521      ME3       $58,136
                    1385      ME3       $61,460
```

```
                        AIRLINE.PAYROLLCHANGES Table

             Emp                Job                     DateOf      DateOf
              ID    Gender      Code     Salary         Birth        Hire

             1639     F         TA3      $59,164      30JUN1955   31JAN1982
             1065     M         ME3      $53,326      29JAN1942   10JAN1985
             1561     M         TA3      $51,120      03DEC1961   10OCT1985
             1221     F         FA3      $41,854      25SEP1965   07OCT1989
             1447     F         FA1      $30,972      11AUG1970   01NOV2000
```

```
                        AIRLINE.PAYROLLMASTER Table

             Emp                Job                     DateOf      DateOf
              ID    Gender      Code     Salary         Birth        Hire

             1919     M         TA2      $48,126      16SEP1958   07JUN1985
             1653     F         ME2      $49,151      19OCT1962   12AUG1988
             1400     M         ME1      $41,677      08NOV1965   19OCT1988
             1350     F         FA3      $46,040      04SEP1963   01AUG1988
             1401     M         TA3      $54,351      16DEC1948   21NOV1983
```

AIRLINE.STAFFCHANGES Table

Emp ID	LastName	First Name	City	State	PhoneNumber
1639	CARTER	KAREN	STAMFORD	CT	203/781-8839
1065	CHAPMAN	NEIL	NEW YORK	NY	718/384-5618
1561	SANDERS	RAYMOND	NEW YORK	NY	212/588-6615
1221	WALTERS	DIANE	NEW YORK	NY	718/384-1918
1447	BRIDESTON	AMY	NEW YORK	NY	718/384-1213

AIRLINE.STAFFMASTER Table

Emp ID	LastName	First Name	City	State	PhoneNumber
1919	ADAMS	GERALD	STAMFORD	CT	203/781-1255
1653	ALEXANDER	SUSAN	BRIDGEPORT	CT	203/675-7715
1400	APPLE	TROY	NEW YORK	NY	212/586-0808
1350	ARTHUR	BARBARA	NEW YORK	NY	718/383-1549
1401	AVERY	JERRY	PATERSON	NJ	201/732-8787

AIRLINE.SUPERVISORS Table

Emp ID	State	Job Category
1677	CT	BC
1834	NY	BC
1431	CT	FA
1433	NJ	FA
1983	NY	FA

Appendix D Index